THE
VOLUNTEER'S

FIELD GUIDE
TO
Youth Ministry

PRACTICAL WAYS TO MAKE A
PERMANENT DIFFERENCE IN
TEENAGERS'
LIVES

BY LEN KAGELER

"THOSE ABOVE"

OTHER VOLUNTEERS

PARENTS

TEENAGERS

YOUTH WORK

YOU!

The Volunteer's Field Guide to Youth Ministry
Practical Ways to Make a Permanent Difference in Teenagers' Lives

group.com
simplyyouthministry.com

Credits
Author: Leonard Kageler
Executive Developer: Nadim Najm
Chief Creative Officer: Joani Schultz
Editors: Michael Novelli and Rob Cunningham
Cover Art and Production: Riley Hall
Production Manager: DeAnne Lear

Library of Congress Cataloging-in-Publication Data
Kageler, Len, 1950-
  The volunteer's field guide to youth ministry : practical ways to make a permanent difference in teenagers / Len Kageler.
     p. cm.
  Includes bibliographical references and index.
  ISBN 978-0-7644-4682-5 (pbk.)
 1. Church group work with youth. 2. Church group work with teenagers. 3. Christian leadership. 4. Voluntarism--Religious aspects--Christianity. I. Title.
  BV4447.K3525 2011
  259'.23--dc22
                                              2011002836

ISBN 978-0-7644-4682-5

10 9 8 7 6 5 4 3 2 1   20 19 18 17 16 15 14 13 12 11

Printed in the United States of America.

CONTENTS

PART 1
THE TERRAIN: YOU!

PART 2
THE TERRAIN: THE "FIELD" OF YOUTH WORK

PART 3
THE WILDLIFE: TEENAGERS

PART 4

THE WILDLIFE: PARENTS

PART 5
THE WILDLIFE: OTHER VOLUNTEERS

PART 6
THE WILDLIFE: "THOSE ABOVE"

PREFACE

All in all, last Wednesday night went pretty well. On the 15-minute drive to church, I recall thinking, "I'm so tired tonight; I wish I could just stay home," and I recall praying, "OK, Lord. I do love these students, and I know you do, too. Will *you* please show up tonight?" Fellow volunteers Stephanie and Paul did a great job leading the two games (an indoor baseball game, and a mutation of Freeze Tag), and the Bible study before refreshments (Mrs. Hobb's cookies were great!) went pretty well, too. We looked at the last bit of Philippians, talking about what it means to be generous and kind to others. We turned off the lights, lit a candle (as we always do), and gathered the group around it for prayer time. I asked the students to thank God for something in prayer. Of the all teenagers present, only two said "pass," and the rest sincerely prayed their own expressions of gratitude for knowing God.

I'm a volunteer in youth ministry. I'm the "Director" of our middle school (ages 11-13) youth group ministry in our small-sized church. Average attendance on Wednesday nights: 10. Average amount of time I can carve out per week for serving our youth group, including Wednesday night: three or four hours. Yep, I know there is more I could do, but by God's grace I do what I can in the time I have.

I've been doing youth ministry in some form or another for many years. Admittedly, I'm an unusual volunteer in that I used to be a youth pastor and now teach youth ministry at a Christian college. But I'm a volunteer nonetheless, and this is my first time to lead a youth group that is a non-white majority. I've been on a steep learning curve. For example, I recruited a student leadership team of four teenagers: two Caucasians, one Cambodian, and one Chinese. No one told me Cambodian and Chinese teenagers raised in fairly traditional homes don't make eye contact with adults who aren't family members. The lack of eye contact is a sign of respect, but I had expected them to share ideas, give feedback, and become almost equal partners with me in the planning functions of leadership. At first, they would hardly even speak! Needless to say, I'm learning a lot in this volunteer role!

This book is meant to be a *field guide*, as in "a portable illustrated book to help identify birds, plants, and rocks." Wait—not birds, plants, and rocks, but youth work in all its varied facets.

I had some help in writing this book: Nearly 700 other volunteers completed an online Volunteer Youth Workers Survey answering 25 questions about themselves and their youth ministry experiences. You'll see some of their input and advice in the sidebars. When it comes to youth ministry volunteering, the Top Five Frustrations and the Top Five Joys of these youth workers are addressed in these pages. Respondents included Roman Catholic (16 percent), Mainline (40 percent), Conservative/Evangelical (34 percent) and Other (10 percent). In the book, when I refer to "the survey," this is the one I'm talking about.

You are welcome to read this field guide from front to back, but it has also been written to be a kind of reference tool…you can scan for subjects you need help with *right now* and save the rest for later. You'll see topics are grouped into larger categories. You'll find sections on "The Terrain" (concerning you) and "The Wildlife" (concerning students, parents, and other important groups).

I promise to be open about my own ministry mistakes and even catastrophes. Others have agreed also to share less than shining ministry moments. Most of us find it comforting to see how others have messed up.

I hope you'll find *The Volunteer's Field Guide to Youth Ministry* encouraging, helpful, and even fun. Youth ministry is an adventure, after all, one that is connected to the kingdom in a wonderful way. So dive in!

THE TERRAIN

You!

In part one of this guide we will focus on two major things: (1) you as a person and (2) "the field" of youth work. You are a wonderful, complex, committed, and imperfect person full of strengths and a few weaknesses as well. Understand yourself and understand this terrain, and you'll likely enjoy and understand "the field" of youth ministry as a volunteer all the more...and see more good things as a result.

CHAPTER 1

BALANCING ACTS

> ### One of the top five frustrations volunteer youth workers share: "I'm so busy with the rest of my life, sometimes it's overwhelming to try to be with teenagers, too."
> #### –Volunteer Youth Workers Survey

I was running around the last couple of days before the retreat like the proverbial chicken with its head cut off...trying to fit in time to finish all the details: things I was supposed to be ready to do (like lead the whole thing, including giving four inspiring messages) and things I should have delegated to someone else (like arranging transportation, planning the meal menu, and shopping for the food). I was an adrenaline-filled crazy man, and finally my wife burst into tears, saying, "We can't go on like this!"

Hmmm.

Being overwhelmed in life has lots of causes, of course. In my case, it was my own disorganization, procrastination, and misguided sense of "I can do it better myself" that caused those around me to shake their heads in bafflement or disgust.

"THOSE ABOVE"

OTHER VOLUNTEERS

PARENTS

TEENAGERS

YOUTH WORK

YOU!

3

We all survived the retreat, though just barely, and I purposed in my heart to "never again" follow the path of disorganization and procrastination.

Chances are you're busy, right? Yes, it is not just people who live in New York City, San Francisco, and Chicago. People in Waco, Texas, Puyallup, Washington, and Manchester, Vermont, feel busy, too. Ideas abound as to why this is, but I'm sure a big reason has to do with technology and its radical transformation of our experience of time. We can all relate to the idea that technology tends to make multitaskers of all of us. We drive while texting and listening to a British-accented GPS woman telling us, "turn right...recallibrating... turn left." We feel bad if we don't answer a text message within 15 seconds. We listen to Pandora®, watch a movie or football game with the sound on "mute," and work on our income taxes simultaneously. We feel ill at ease if we are offline or out of cell coverage.

I've observed that whenever we get new technology that saves us time, we tend to *add* more activity or responsibility, rather than use that "saved" time for relaxation or personal deepening. The result? We have very little margin in our lives, and if something goes wrong or even just takes longer than we think it should, all of a sudden we're feeling crowded, tight, even out of control.

Here are four practical ideas that may reduce the sense of "I'm overwhelmed."

1. **Brain Boundaries**
   This may be difficult at first, but realize your body can't pump adrenaline all the time. That can actually lead to adrenaline addiction, and if our body is "on alert" all the time it may eventually result in the collapse of the body's immune system.[1]

You have to have some downtime…for reflection, processing, and just inhabiting your own life-world. Be radical; at least once a day, purposely walk slower. No kidding…you'll be surprised the feeling you get—even if your walk is just from your car to the grocery store. As a matter of habit, slow down and give your brain some space.

2. Calendar Boundaries

Your youth ministry work is never quite done, right? There is always one more teenager to connect with on Facebook®, one more parent to affirm, one more…you fill in the blank. I try to limit my youth ministry volunteering work to two evenings (or partial evenings) a week. I might think of something on another night that should be done, but I just make a note of it and save it for one of the two nights.

3. Lived Moments

When do you feel most alive? Is it hearing your 3-year-old daughter say, "I love you, mommy"? sitting in your favorite coffee shop talking with a friend? playing your guitar? planning your next trip? At the end of each day, I try to think back and recall when I felt most alive, and thank God for those moments.
This next idea may seem a bit bizarre and I'm not saying this is an "ought" for everyone, but it does help me keep long-term perspective on my life and see God's long-term presence as well. Every week I take a few minutes and write down in a journal when I felt most alive in the previous seven days. It is a journal of my lived moments. If there are big problems or issues going on, they get written down, too. For those areas I try to practice 1 Peter 5:7: *Give all your worries and cares to God, for he cares about you.* I have been making these weekly journal entries since 1983.

"THOSE ABOVE"

OTHER VOLUNTEERS

PARENTS

TEENAGERS

YOUTH WORK

YOU!

> *"Having to work full time to support my family, pay for everything that I do for the youth group, and be able to give the time to the youth that I feel they deserve...sometimes it just stretches me too thin."*
>
> *–Volunteer from rural Texas*

And here is the fun part. In the first few days of every month I look back in the journal to what I wrote in *that month* 25 years ago, 20 years ago, 15, 10, and 5. I write some of the highlights and share them with my wife and now-adult daughters. We sometimes laugh at the great memories. We thank God that in the many crises and hard times, we found God's grace and presence to be sufficient.

All in all, these "lived moment" practices help me, particularly in hard times, to remember that God's long-term hand was with me in the past, is present with me now, and will be with me in the future. In some weird way this practice acts kind of like a vaccine against an "overwhelmed" state of mind.

4. **Family-Life Sanity**

   If you are a parent and your children are school age, *you are not obligated to schedule every waking moment of your child's life* with lessons, sports, personal coaching, and other wonderful activities to enrich their lives and secure their future. And furthermore, you are *not* obligated to taxi your children to all these activities, and you are *not* obligated, as a good parent, to show up at every rehearsal, performance, practice, and game to "be there" for them.

Now, put down that stone you're about to throw at me! I'm not saying your child shouldn't take violin lessons or sign up for the basketball team. I'm not saying you shouldn't go to (many of) the games. All I'm saying is that I've seen too many well-meaning parents who run themselves to near insanity careening like a ball in a pinball machine through each day as they try to build their son or daughter's portfolio.

> *"I love being with the kids and always have fun at get-togethers and events. It's just a matter of the time it takes away from my family that can sometimes be difficult."*
>
> *–Volunteer from urban Iowa*

I live in a context (New York City and its environs) where parents have tremendous angst about what *preschool* their children will attend...they're willing to "network" like crazy to get a "pre-application interview" and then, if that goes well, plunk down $40,000 for the tuition to the preschool that boasts the highest admission rates to Harvard University. (No, I'm not making this up.) To these parents it is all about shaping, balancing, and enhancing

"THOSE ABOVE"

OTHER VOLUNTEERS

PARENTS

TEENAGERS

YOUTH WORK

YOU!

children's life experiences so they will be most marketable to the Ivy League.

There is a body of social science research that has begun to show it's possible to "over parent." For example, some studies are revealing that one of the greatest contributors to a child's development is "imaginative play" in which children have time to figure out how to occupy themselves happily with minimal adult intervention.[2] This kind of play can be a wonderful contributor to a child's development. Yet in our culture, adolescence seems to be extending into the mid- to late 20s. It seems that many adolescents have been protected from making important choices for the first 18 to 22 years of their lives. Some experts suggest this insolated environment actually is altering the brain wiring of adolescents, in part caused by watchful, protective, and well-intentioned parenting.[3]

> ## "It's OK to say no when you are too busy."
> ### –Volunteer from suburban Ohio

I'm not saying your children shouldn't be involved in extra-curricular activities, but tuba in the marching band, lead role in the high school musical, basketball team, Kung Fu lessons, and community soccer league play…all simultaneously? *Are you crazy?* If you are a parent, ask yourself, "Do I feel run-ragged by the various activities my kids are in?" If your answer is yes, one step in addressing the "overwhelmed" feeling in your life may be taking another look at your children's list of activities and how that impacts your own life and the life of your family.

CALLING

"THOSE ABOVE"

OTHER VOLUNTEERS

PARENTS

TEENAGERS

YOUTH WORK

YOU!

Do you have a sense of calling to volunteer in youth ministry? What I mean by "calling" is that you have sensed a *divine intention* that you should be working with students. You feel drawn to the teenagers by God, and it is a meaningful way for you to serve and invest. A sense of calling keeps us going when times are hard for us personally and for us in ministry. We sense that God's purpose and strength are with us and will help us to persevere.

> *"By joining the team of youth leaders, it has changed my life and my priorities. These kids have given me a purpose to seek, and I will forever be grateful to God for giving me such an awesome, breathtaking task of life."*
> *–Volunteer from rural Oregon*

A few weeks ago, youth group meeting had started (nine students present) and was going fine until five boys walked in, having just been kicked out of the library two blocks away. They knew a couple of girls in the group and were there to harass and tease them and generally have a good time. (Of course, they had their own definition of "good time." Picture your own church, say, with 300 people present when 150 extra people show up whose only intention is to disrupt. That's what this felt like.) We managed to make it through the rest of the evening without injury to students or the building, but it was iffy some of the time as one guy threw Christmas lights at others and constantly denied it when confronted, while another rummaged through the church kitchen, helping himself to whatever he liked. During the "serious time" of the evening they interrupted, disrupted, and bullied the others present. I was pretty discouraged when I headed home, wondering if we'd face this battle for control every week. It was a sense of *divine intention* that helped Paul, Steph, and me process what took place and face the future with a desire to keep going.

In the Bible there are basically two ways people feel a "call."

In the Old Testament, calling is most definitely a "from on high" experience. Think of Abraham, minding his own wealthy business when God showed up and informed him the time had come for him, his family, and his flock to experience a permanent change of address (Genesis 12:1). We don't have a DVD or YouTube® clip of this event, but it is still easy for us to imagine that the first reaction of his wife, family, and multitude of servants was not "Sounds great, Abe. Let's call our Internet provider, cable company, and 30 other people we do business with and just tell 'em to forward the final bills to...where?"

Think of poor Gideon, surreptitiously (for fear of the occupying army of Midian) minding his own organic multigrain processing facility when an angel appeared to him with the words *"Mighty hero, the Lord is with you!" (Judges 6:12)*. Gideon's response was not "Well, it's nice that God finally recognizes my innate talents" or "At your service, oh mighty angel who interrupts my workday!" Rather,

Gideon launched into a tirade of complaints to God about the abandonment of Israel. God's call to Gideon was to lead an army of insurrection—a call that was both divine and menacing.

I find that some youth workers have this same sort of sense of call to volunteer in youth work. In the survey, I asked, "Why are you doing youth work?" Some of the answers included:

- *"Couldn't imagine doing anything else, even if the calling is a love/hate thing."*
- *"To have a deep burden, a heart that bleeds for youth and their needs."*
- *"A leading of God toward teenagers that is a persistent knocking."*
- *"God places a burden on your heart for teenagers."*

In the New Testament, "calling" is expressed quite differently. It's mainly in the context of the believing community, where "spiritual gifts" are expressed (see Chapter 4) and where this giftedness is recognized and affirmed by others. The Apostle Paul states, *In his grace, God has given us different gifts for doing certain things well (Romans 12:6).* For some, youth work is a perfect way to express spiritual giftedness when combined with the right opportunity. When asked "Why are you doing youth work?" some answers included:

- *"Recognizing giftedness and ability."*
- *"Receiving direction and commendation from God-honoring mentors, friends, elders, and pastors."*
- *"Asking the Spirit for direction...and maybe being available and willing to meet a current youth ministry need and thereby 'falling' into it."*
- *"Going through doors God produces for you."*
- *"God has prepared me to be in this work. I feel God's pleasure in me being in this work."*

"THOSE ABOVE"

OTHER VOLUNTEERS

PARENTS

TEENAGERS

YOUTH WORK

YOU!

Whether you got into youth ministry through an on-high call, through giftedness and opportunity, or perhaps because at the church's annual meeting you raised your hand to ask a question without realizing the subject had moved from the church budget to who will teach junior high boys Sunday school—whatever the path, you probably see that God has something to do with it.

PERSONALITY 4

"THOSE ABOVE"

OTHER VOLUNTEERS

PARENTS

TEENAGERS

YOUTH WORK

YOU!

Understanding your personality

Personality differences have been a subject of curiosity and speculation for millennia. Hippocrates began the identifying distinctions in personality 2,500 years ago, and today, temperament theory receives much academic attention. A few decades ago it was common to recognize temperament differences as simply the result of upbringing and environment. Today, however, many researchers see a strong biologic determinant in how our personalities are shaped.

We're different because we were created different. Why would God want people to be different? One doesn't have to be a theologian to understand that each person is to have a different function in the body of Christ. The teaching of Scripture on spiritual gifts is clear about this (see Ephesians 4, 1 Corinthians 12, and Romans 12).

We see personality differences all around us. My three daughters have very different personalities. The students in my junior high group are amazingly different. Members of our volunteer staff are quite different. This is great! Some of our teenagers connect best with Steph, some with Paul, some with me, and so on.

My favorite way of explaining personality differences is by using the labels Lions, Otters, Golden Retrievers, and Ants.[5]

Lions are leaders and can be aggressive. They like to make decisions and make things happen. They are wired to be confident about themselves and their decisions. They don't require much information to make a decision and don't need much feedback as to how they are doing a particular task.

Otters are the life-of-the-party, fun-loving "people persons" who love to make wide social contacts. They are spontaneous, dynamic, and feel energized when entering a room full of strangers. The pastor of the church I attend has some otter in him; he loves to make people laugh in person and in his sermons.

Golden Retrievers are deeply relational and sensitive. They love to get inside the head and heart of another person. They love to care and be cared for. They love to listen to the deep needs of others.

Ants love to be factual, organized, and analytical. They make decisions comfortably only when they have all the facts in front of them. They work hard and do things right.

"THOSE ABOVE"

OTHER VOLUNTEERS

PARENTS

TEENAGERS

YOUTH WORK

YOU!

> ## "I am a behind-the-scenes person. I like to organize and be a gopher that makes things happen."
> *–Volunteer from suburban Indiana*

Most youth workers I've met have a personality centered in one or two of these areas. In the survey, respondents were asked to name their one main personality type.

- Lions—35 percent
- Otters—18 percent
- Golden Retrievers—27 percent
- Ants—20 percent

To better understand the four personality styles, imagine four different rooms. Let's walk into a room full of ants. It's a quiet but happy room. Ants don't require a lot of social interaction. Some ants will be talking quietly and seriously; others will be saying nothing at all; and some ants will have a brought a book or notebook computer along to make the best use of their time. Ants are content without a party.

Now come into a room full of golden retrievers. The noise level is higher because these golden retrievers enjoy interacting so much. They are sharing, listening, and are very focused. They enjoy getting to know each other deeply. If the building were burning down, they may not notice, being so in tune with listening to and sharing deeply with each other.

If you dare, come into a room full of otters; it's party time! In this room otters are laughing, joking around, and clearly enjoying one another. Paper airplanes sail across the room and (look out!)

someone brought a stash of water guns. Otters love action and would rather not be alone. Otters feel responsible to help everyone have a good time. They are driven to help everyone smile and enjoy.

Let's go now to the only room I hesitate to show you. It is the only unhappy room of the four. You see, lions are uncomfortable until they figure out which of them is the main lion. Until that is sorted out, there can be some terse exchanges, one-upmanship talk, and verbal sparring to see who gets the high ground.

It is not hard to see how these four personality types differ when it comes to job satisfaction. Lions are happiest when in charge of something or someone. They like to manage, give orders, and make decisions. Otters make great salespeople. Don't put an otter behind a desk for long because she or he will want to be out with people. Golden retrievers make great customer service representatives. Even if you're angry when you call, they will make you feel as if they've been waiting all day just to listen to your pain. Years ago, I made just such a call about my Ford Taurus, which has long since passed on to glory. The golden retriever on the other end listened to my pain, acknowledged my frustration, and kindly let me know Ford wouldn't do a single thing for me. Despite the bad news, when the conversation was over, I actually felt good about the call and about Ford. At least they heard my pain!

Ants make great accountants, actuaries, programmers, library acquisition personnel, and technical writers. Facing a day of minimal human contact is no problem to them! It's energizing, not draining.

Let's talk about relationships between these personality types. Lion and otter types tend to marry golden retriever and ants. Lions find the sensitive golden retrievers so mysterious, so unfathomable, and so alluring. Golden retrievers, on the other hand, are amazed at the confidence, direction, and outspokenness of lions. Unfortunately, what is so mysterious and wonderful in the warm glow of pre-honeymoon attraction can be downright irritating a few years— even weeks—later. (Computer-based matching services, such as eHarmony.com, are largely personality-based. Their premise is this: People who are more similar have a vastly better chance of finding joy, fulfillment, and a lasting marriage.)

Do we find these creatures (personality types) in the Bible? Although they are not listed along with the gifts of the Spirit, personality differences are described throughout the Bible. Paul and Peter seemed to be very lion-like. Was Andrew an otter? Friendship evangelism has been called *Operation Andrew* by the Billy Graham Evangelistic Association. How about Mary and Martha? Luke 10 reveals Martha as the organized ant and Mary as the soak-it-all-in golden retriever. I think Nehemiah was a combination of lion and ant. There's a combination that can get something done!

Let's take a look at how these personality types relate to youth ministry volunteering.

Good news for all types

It is encouraging to know that God uses all kinds of people in youth work! His calling is not limited to lions only, or any one type. If we think about Jesus' selection of his closest disciples, we are reminded that he chose a variety of personalities who would eventually be let loose to turn the world upside down.

Let's consider the strengths of each personality type as it pertains to a vital youth ministry.

"THOSE ABOVE"

OTHER VOLUNTEERS

PARENTS

TEENAGERS

YOUTH WORK

YOU!

Lions have no hesitation about standing up in front of groups. To lead a youth ministry someone has to be up there, right? Many people fear speaking in front of others more than they fear death. Well, lions don't have this problem. Lions are great at providing direction, vision, and a sense that this youth ministry is going places. They don't get bogged down with decision making. It would not take a lion long to decide whether to do an evangelistic mission trip, help build a house with Habitat for Humanity, or both.

My survey included this question: "Are you the 'chief' volunteer? That is, do you supervise other volunteers?" It's no surprise that the majority of "chief" volunteers are lions (46 percent). The other personality types were far behind (golden retriever at 23 percent, ant at 18 percent, and otter at 14 percent).

There is much in a lion that is attractive to teenagers. They like a sense of purpose and direction. They want meaning. Lions are great when it comes to "telling it like it is," leading students into meaningful challenges, and helping them experience for themselves the joy of making a difference. Parents and church leaders tend to have confidence in a ministry led with vision and purpose.

I'm not sure what got into me, but I once read a 500-page book with the title *Sociology of Leisure*. Well, otters don't need a book to understand fun! Otters want to have a good time, but their desire is not selfish. They want others to have a good time as well. In youth work, otters are the kinds of people who make teenagers smile, laugh, and go home exclaiming, "That was awesome!" Otters love to have fun, be it a spontaneous trip to Pizza Hut or a long-planned sports outreach event.

Otters make great youth workers because they want to make sure every single student who walks in the door feels important. Otters work hard to create a positive atmosphere that attracts teenagers and makes them feel comfortable.

Students are attracted to otters because they're attracted to life. An otter-led youth ministry is one in which teenagers feel good about the group and their involvement in it. They enjoy bringing friends because they know their friends will have a good time and hear a positive message.

Youth ministry is a job made in heaven for golden retrievers. Adolescence is a stormy time, and teenagers frequently struggle with insecurities, hurts, and difficulties. Golden retrievers provide support for them. The gift of time and listening are blessings that a golden retriever brings to a youth ministry. They are concerned that the personal needs of teenagers are being met.

Golden retrievers are especially good at hanging out before and after a meeting or event. I have seen teenagers and golden retrievers standing around talking in the parking lot long after the youth room is cleaned up, the lights are off, and the doors are locked.

Students are attracted to golden retriever-led youth groups because they know they have a friend. Programs do not bring people; people bring people. The connectedness teenagers feel to the golden retrievers in a youth ministry ensure their return again and again and again.

Ants can also make great youth workers. Some of our students are ants, too, and they can immediately sense when the leader is one of their own. Ants are never sloppy in their organization of the youth ministry. Teenagers and parents know that if it appears on the youth calendar, it is going to happen and all details will be covered. The event, the ministry will flow because the myriad of details needed

"THOSE ABOVE"

OTHER VOLUNTEERS

PARENTS

TEENAGERS

YOUTH WORK

YOU!

to run a youth ministry are both understood and handled eagerly by ants. Ants keep people informed, they don't lose money, and their word is good.

Ants can be masters at one-to-one discipling, not only mentoring in spiritual truth, but also mentoring via modeling. I know ant youth workers who find teenagers to share their hobbies. Fishing, model boat building, and remote control aircraft flying are great arenas in which the gospel can be nurtured in a young heart. Quality time is often a function of quantity time, and ants are very creative in finding areas where time can be invested in ministry.

Students like ants because they like stability, trustworthiness, and excellence. Many appreciate the one-on-one emphasis that is all too absent in many homes.

A few years back, I did research about personality style and numerical growth in youth ministry. All types of personalities were associated in some way with growing youth ministries.

Percentage of 500 Youth Ministries Whose Main Meeting Saw a Numerical Increase Over the Previous Two Years

Main Personality Type of Youth Pastor	Leading a Middle School Group (% whose group grew over 2 years)	Leading a Senior High Group (% whose group grew over 2 years)
Ant	74%	48%
Golden Retriever	62%	54%
Otter	66%	59%
Lion	81%	69%

We see here that every personality style can be associated with numerical growth. Yes, some settings are more optimal than others, but God can use you in ministry. It's even better if all four personality styles can be represented by members of your volunteer team.

Each personality has potential for positive outcomes in a youth ministry. There are, however, potential downsides to each personality type. Lions can tend to be insensitive, making rash decisions and causing people to feel their opinions don't matter. Otters are known to be disorganized, poorly prepared, and lacking in follow-through. After all, "it will all work out." Golden retrievers may appear nervous in front of 20 noisy junior highers. All the planning required to run a youth ministry can also seem like a crushing burden to them. Ants may not attract many teenage otters, since ants find it difficult to project enthusiasm in the group setting.

Know who you are
Aside from your own spiritual formation, understanding your personality is one of the most crucial insights youth workers need to flourish.

Some may contest that personality typing is just another means for labeling people and unnecessarily generalizing in ways that are possibly damaging. I grant that people are complex and may behave in different ways in different circumstances. I also understand there are a zillion different personality profiles out there. But gaining insight into our personalities and tendencies helps us to better understand who are and how we might best serve God.

"THOSE ABOVE"

OTHER VOLUNTEERS

PARENTS

TEENAGERS

YOUTH WORK

YOU!

> *If you are interested in the brain research side of all this, Galen's Prophecy by Harvard researcher Jerome Kagan may convince you that personality tendencies are hard wired into us before birth and this hard wiring has profound implications on individual human development.*[6]

One great thing about knowing yourself is that you know what you do well. When we do what it seems like we are born to do, it's like we can hear God singing over us with the same joy prophesied in Zephaniah 3:17. As a "lion/otter" I'm good at creating a positive, affirming, fun environment. I'm good at leading leaders. I'm driven to affirm and build youth and youth workers. On the other hand, I'm terrible at counseling. Ask me to set up a six-session counseling schedule with a teenager (or a parent), and my heart will sink and I'll dread every meeting. Ask me to have a deep conversation with a teenager in need in the midst of 10 or 50 other teenagers around and it's like you're asking me the impossible. I'm so driven to meet/greet/make-everyone-feel-good in the room that focusing on one person seems unnatural to me. Some of you are thinking, "Yes, that's exactly how I feel," while others are saying, "I can't believe he can't do what every youth worker *should* be able to do." Speaking of *shoulds*...

Realize other personality styles are not wrong, just different
I nearly drove a God-honoring and gifted youth ministry intern insane by my expectation that he take youth to lunch from school

during the week. I took students to lunch routinely. Most schools in my area had a 31-minute lunch break. I could pick the person up (or, if a girl, plus one or two friends), take them to a nearby fast food place, eat lunch, and have them back to campus with two minutes to spare. On the way back to school I would always ask them if there was anything I could pray for them about, and if the answer was longer than a couple minutes, we'd talk on the phone after school or in the evening.

My intern, Jim, told me over and over again, with stress written all over his face, he just couldn't have a 31-minute lunch with a teenager. For the longest time I just couldn't understand why he couldn't get with it, measure up, and get motivated to do this incredibly simple and easy (to me) task.

It finally hit me one evening after youth group, when and I saw Jim talking deeply with a few students. I reflected on what he said was the best thing in youth ministry for him: *getting deep with teenagers*. I finally had this epiphany: *Jim is different than me, and it's OK!* He nearly wept with joy when I affirmed that he was really good at having deep conversations with teenagers and that I no longer expected him to do short lunch appointments with them.

This experience led to another epiphany: All of my volunteers (there were 30 at the time) were wired to be very good at something. *I should figure out what they are good at and unleash them to do it.*

Now perhaps this is all elementary to you, but it changed my life and ministry. Ultimately, it meant I gave (and still do give) the lion-otter personality test to all the other volunteers.

I wanted lions to be in charge of something from time to time.

I made sure my otters led games or planned fun stuff on retreats.

I gathered lots of golden retrievers, did not expect them to stand in front of the youth group (ever), and made sure they were in small groups with students.

I made sure to assign administrative or detail-oriented projects and tasks to any ant on the team.

As you might expect, people got very happy. They were being empowered, not enslaved in youth ministry.

Don't quit work—network
The key to overcoming the weakness inherent in our personalities is networking. First, we need to network with God. The recognition of our glaring weaknesses forces us to get on our knees and acknowledge that God is our source of strength, hope, and effectiveness.

Recently, one of my junior highers came to me and poured out his heart. He was in the middle of a personal crisis and needed care. Internally I panicked, but as I prayerfully settled down, I was able to be used by God in this student's life. All I did was listen and acknowledge that I agreed that what he was experiencing was both hard and disappointing. I affirmed I would pray for him and phone him in a couple of days to see how it was going. I was weak, but in God's strength I was able to function.

This kind of spiritual exchange—human weakness for God's strength—takes place continually in our lives as we submit to God's ways. Lions find themselves in counseling situations, otters are writing up the summer camp reports for the elder board, golden retrievers are leading the "shuffle your buns" game, and ants are trying to keep 15 wiggly students from climbing out of the windows during Sunday school. Sometimes we find ourselves functioning in areas where we are not strong, but we thank God for his grace and for the others who are filling out the whole personality picture with us.

Networking with God is crucial; so is networking with others in youth ministry. We need people who are not like ourselves to work alongside us in ministry; lions especially need golden retrievers to provide the personal care students so desperately need. Otters are in critical need of ants who can handle the details. Golden retrievers need otters and lions who don't mind being in front of the group. Ants need otters to create the positive and fun atmosphere so essential to a growing youth ministry.

There can be amazing joy in all of this. As we understand our God-given personalities, we are set free to serve him in enthusiastic joy.

"THOSE ABOVE"

OTHER VOLUNTEERS

PARENTS

TEENAGERS

YOUTH WORK

YOU!

CHAPTER 4

SPIRITUAL GIFTS

I *love* to teach about spiritual gifts, even to junior high school students. Christians have various understandings and interpretations about spiritual gifts, but I try to keep to the basics. Spiritual gifts are not to be confused with the *gift* of the Holy Spirit we encounter in Trinitarian theology, as one of the three persons of God (Father, Son, Holy Spirit). They are also not to be confused with the *fruit* of the Spirit we see in Galatians 5:22-23, which is the outworking or evidence of one's growing relationship with Christ (love, joy, peace, patience, and so on). Rather, spiritual gifts are particular empowerments or abilities for ministry. In Scripture we see that every Christian has at least one spiritual gift (see 1 Corinthians 12) and that the purpose of each spiritual gift is to contribute to and build up the Christian community, the church (Ephesians 4:12)

One way I like to illustrate this when teaching this to teenagers is to have one of the volunteer leaders (I'll call him Jamal) lie down on a very large sheet of paper before the meeting. I trace the outline of this person, draw in some clothes and other details, and cut the figure into the same number of pieces as students I expect to show up to the youth group meeting. Students each get a "piece" as they enter and are asked to keep it handy. I have selected students read the key texts and explain what they think the passage means.

I then ask, "Does anyone have any idea what you were given when you came in tonight?"

"THOSE ABOVE"

OTHER VOLUNTEERS

PARENTS

TEENAGERS

YOUTH WORK

YOU!

Someone will eventually say, "It looks like a puzzle piece" or "I think this is an ear."

I then say, "You're both right...IT'S JAMAL! You each have a piece of him, and now you have three minutes to put him together. GO!

Panadmonium then ensues. Jamal looks on and loudly complains if he has a foot growing out of his head or if anything else is a little off.

When the pieces of Jamal are all reassembled, I interview him to ask how he feels now that he is all back together. I then pick up (for example) the left knee.

"How well could you get along without this, my friend?" He might say he could get along without his left knee.

"Show me." Jamal tries to walk or, more likely, hop on one leg.

"Well, how about without your right foot?" I pick the piece up and put it in my pocket. "Jamal, show us how you'd get around now." Chances are, he'd now crawl on his stomach.

"Just stay there for another minute...how well could you get along without this?" I then take all the puzzle pieces related to and including his head. On this cue, Jamal gets up and runs out of the room.

I then have the same students who read the spiritual gift passages at the beginning read them again. Then I ask, "So, what's the point?"

You know, they get it. They see Jamal needs all of him. If he's missing something, it's hard to function.

This makes a great introduction to the topic of spiritual gifts, and by this time students are ready to learn about the specific ones.

> *"I LOVE being able to teach the Bible study. I LOVE being able to keep things organized and running smoothly. I LOVE to hang out with the kids and help them work through a problem by 'problem solving' and seeing the joy on their faces when they understand they can work through a problem and solve it in a non-confrontational way."*
>
> *–Volunteer from rural New York*

Three primary texts in the New Testament list spiritual gifts: Ephesians 4:11 (apostleship, prophecy, evangelism, and pastor/teacher) describes foundational or general gifts within the whole body of Christ; Romans 12:6-8 (preaching, serving, teaching, encouragement, giving, leadership, and mercy) lists specific-working gifts; and 1 Corinthians 12:28 provides the additional gifts of miracles, healing, administration, and tongues.[7]

The concept of spiritual gifts can be incredibly helpful in youth work. First, it's just plain encouraging seeing oneself as gifted. Second, if I know what my spiritual gifts are and also understand

"THOSE ABOVE"

OTHER VOLUNTEERS

PARENTS

TEENAGERS

YOUTH WORK

YOU!

the giftedness of those around me, we can be a much better team in working together.

I really enjoy seeing spiritual gifts in teenagers. Among the ones I see the most are mercy and service. My students who are merciful care deeply about others and look for ways to help, support, and encourage people who are in pain or difficulty. I've seen otherwise reluctant or reticent students come alive in the context of visiting the pediatric section of a hospital or a cerebral palsy center. Of course, we all are supposed to be caring and merciful, but some seem to have this in a supernatural measure. Students who have the gift of services are wonderful to have around. They come alive when given the chance to set up that media equipment, arrange refreshment tables, or clean up after that pizza or marshmallow melee.

What might the spiritual gifts listed in the Romans 12 passage look like for those of us who volunteer in youth ministry?

Those with the spiritual gift of service find real joy in doing the behind-the-scenes tasks that make the more public things go smoothly. Yes, of course, we all need to be willing to do what most would consider mundane, like setting up chairs or cleaning out the church van after a trip. But people with the gift of service may love doing these things. They understand their work, this ministry of service, frees others to use their gifts as well.

The gifts of preaching and teaching show up in people who have at least three qualities: They love preparing to teach, they love the people they teach, and they love teaching in such a way that students understand and experience life change.

Those who have the gift of encouragement (also called exhortation) seem to have the right word and the right time for the right person. Their antennae are up for those who need an understanding heart and a supportive comment. Youth workers with this gift seldom leave a youth event without using this gift. If you have the gift of encouragement, this is one of the highlights of youth ministry… knowing that you're helping students navigate their confusing world.

The gift of giving can be described as the ability to use God's resources wisely. While the biblical context is first related to financial giving to those in need, one can consider "resources" to include time and things. People with this gift love to be generous. In youth ministry it could mean someone letting the youth group (or youth ministry staff) repeatedly use their vacation cabin at no cost. I met one of those people several years ago; we used their Vermont "cabin" for our winter retreats. The place slept 30 students plus staff. On the rental market this cabin can fetch $1,000 per night (no kidding!), but the Gordon family just gave us the keys and said "enjoy." They also insisted that my wife and I come back with family or friends and use it for a week in the summer.

In the Romans passage those with the gift of leadership are encouraged to *take the responsibility seriously*. It seems here we are talking about people who are organized, can plan well, and know how to include others in carrying out these plans.

Mercy describes the joy of volunteers for whom generous forgiveness comes as easily as breathing. If a student is hurting physically or emotionally, those with mercy want to reach out and help.

"THOSE ABOVE"

OTHER VOLUNTEERS

PARENTS

TEENAGERS

YOUTH WORK

YOU!

STRENGTHS

"THOSE ABOVE"

OTHER VOLUNTEERS

PARENTS

TEENAGERS

YOUTH WORK

YOU!

I actually enjoy reading books about leadership or management from time to time, as it seems to me that youth ministry is about leadership, or at least about leading well. In 2001, I came across a book titled *Now, Discover Your Strengths* by Marcus Buckingham and Donald Clifton, and it stood out to me as having a different message. Here is my paraphrase of the main point: Most people are worried about their weaknesses, so they focus their personal development on trying to be stronger in the areas in which they are weak. *Forget about your weaknesses*; focus instead on your strengths. In fact, if the majority of your job doesn't fit with your top five strengths, you're a great candidate for burnout. And speaking of strengths, consider taking the online StrengthsFinder® diagnostic tool; it just might change your life.

Millions have taken the StrengthsFinder® Assessment, logging on to a special website by using an access code provided in each copy of *Now, Discover Your Strengths* (the code is in a sealed envelope and can be used only once). Here is the list of strengths found in this tool: achiever, activator, adaptability, analytical, arranger, belief, command, communication, competition, connectedness, consistency, context, deliberative, developer, discipline, empathy, focus, futuristic, harmony, ideation, includer, individualization, input, intellection, learner, maximizer, positivity, relator, responsibility, restorative, self-assurance, significance, strategic, and woo.[8] You'll find a web link to definitions for each of these strengths in the endnotes of this book.

> Since *Now, Discover Your Strengths* was released in 2001, several additional books and tools have been developed to help people explore and assess their strengths, including *StrengthsExplorer* for teenagers and *StrengthsFinder 2.0*. Go to strengthsfinder.com for more information.

What might this have to do with volunteering in youth ministry? How might this be part of our own personal terrain?

In some ways, discovering our strengths is parallel to personality and spiritual gifts. We should know who we are and how our own (in this case) strengths have an impact on those around us. Not only is it important to know our own strengths, but it's also helpful to know the strengths of those we serve alongside. This insight alone will reduce conflict and lead to more effective ministry.

> *"It is rewarding, I have the opportunity to combine my gifts of administration and compassion, and I enjoy the company of the youth!"*
> –Volunteer from rural Minnesota

For example, I know a full-time youth pastor who was actually fired from his job because he was too competitive. It seemed like all his teaching, all the activities, *everything* related to competition. He loved it, he thrived on it, he saw himself as a winner, and he wanted his students to be winners, too. After all, there are a few sports references and metaphors in Scripture, right? With a little more maturity (and perhaps after taking the StrengthsFinder® test) he might have realized there are dozens of other strengths and most people are not motivated by competition to such a large measure. People strong in "harmony" find competition and anything adversarial (such as choosing sides or being "against" someone) draining at best, debilitating at worst. Add the strengths of command and significance to competition, and some will see a self-absorbed, egotistical, spiritually shallow leader that needs to be replaced ASAP. How I wish someone close to this youth pastor could have pulled him aside to help him see himself as many others saw him.

Even without taking the StrengthsFinder® test, just knowing that *everyone is not like me, and they are not motivated by the same things that motivate me*, is an insight that can lead to more harmony with a group of volunteers.

"THOSE ABOVE"

OTHER VOLUNTEERS

PARENTS

TEENAGERS

YOUTH WORK

YOU!

35

CHAPTER 6

ARE YOU SAD SUSCEPTIBLE?

"THOSE ABOVE"

OTHER VOLUNTEERS

PARENTS

TEENAGERS

YOUTH WORK

YOU!

It was a cool and rainy mid-November Saturday morning. As usual, I had looked forward to the monthly junior high student leadership team meeting. I've always believed teenagers ages 11-13 are much more capable of spiritual growth and leadership than people give them credit for.

After making and eating breakfast together, we moved into a time of prayer and planning the group activities. September and October had gone very well, and great events were on the calendar for us to look forward to. In the two years I'd been at the church, the junior high ministry had grown numerically, but these students also were evidencing they were "getting it" spiritually. Their parents were even noticing the changes in their sons and daughters. I began, "So, before we start planning, how do you feel it's going in the group these days?"

Jana didn't hesitate. "I think it's going terrible. Shella, that new girl, is so obnoxious."

"Yeah, I agree," answered Charlie. "None of the events are any fun anymore."

"I don't even look forward to coming," added Karen.

"I don't like it either, and I think my family might start looking for a different church," Ricci added helpfully.

Believe it or not, the conversation went downhill from there. Negativism was expressed with vehemence and bitter conviction. For me, it was an agonizing hour. When they seemed to be done, I asked, "Does anyone have anything positive, anything good about the group that they want to say?"

Seven pairs of eyes looked back at me. No one responded, not even one. I was so totally blown away that all I could do was close with a brief prayer. After spending the next hour taking all of them home in the church van, I went back to my office and sat at my desk, lost in thought.

"Len, quit being so stupid," I kindly said to myself. "You forgot that it's November."

> *"It is an awesome ministry. It can be emotionally exhausting as you share tears, laughter, and all-around craziness with them. As you see some of them take on their own faith and move out into life as equipped adults, it is pure joy."*
>
> *–Volunteer from urban Colorado*

Here's another example. From time to time I get invited to participate in a youth ministry as an observer, with the idea that I can provide some feedback about issues or help make improvements. Recently I was sitting in on a youth group session that started out bad and got progressively worse. Jennifer began by asking the 25 youth present to "share with us all what God is doing in your life or what you are learning from him these days." Blank stares, silence. "Well, let's sing then!" Jennifer exclaimed as she launched into a song a capella...which continued as a solo. Eventually the teenagers did participate a little bit, but not much. Later that day I met with Jennifer. She was discouraged and devastated that the youth meeting didn't go well. She was even questioning her own call and fitness for ministry, faced with such a spectacular failure.

"Have you ever heard of SAD?" I asked her.

"Yes, of course, but that doesn't really affect teenagers, does it?"

Long pause. "Knowing it is November, there are some things you could have done that would have helped people warm up." It was an epiphany for Jennifer as she realized that even if only a handful of students are "down," their influence can affect how an entire evening goes.

Seasonal Affective Disorder (SAD)...that's a fancy clinical name. In my first few years of ministry I didn't know the clinical name for it, but I did notice a distinct pattern. What I noticed then and still today is that some of the brightest and best people—teenagers and adults—will go into a spiritual tailspin in November. They'll get negative and critical. They won't feel like talking, sharing, or singing.

I used to lie awake at night thinking about this...worrying, praying, wondering why. I tried to use counseling or "heavy" talks with the group or individuals as early weapons. It only took a few years to figure out, however, that no amount of prayer, counseling, or extra meetings would make any difference. All I had to do was wait...by mid- or late December, the grumpy students and adults would snap out of it and be their cheerful and positive selves again.

Seasonal Affective Disorder is well documented both medically and in popular media.[9] Researchers believe that SAD, also called Winter Depression, directly corresponds with shorter amounts of daylight during the winter months. Not only is daylight shorter, but in many areas, winter brings many gray days with overcast weather. This decrease of light level increases the body's production of a chemical called melatonin. In some people, this increase in melatonin seems to produce loss of energy and symptoms of depression—in other words, people get grumpy! For most, six weeks is about what it takes to readjust, though some people have these symptoms throughout the winter months.

Youth workers who don't know about SAD are doubly vulnerable. We are vulnerable first because we're clueless as to why we get blindsided by people who we thought were on our side. Nice, friendly, supportive people all of a sudden want to see our ministries filleted and our souls hung on meat hooks—fodder for the circling vultures they and others have become.

Second, we are vulnerable because we ourselves may be victims of SAD. Things might be going OK and then, without apparent cause or warning, our internal "self-talk" gets negative. We internally rehearse long, critical speeches to our youth group, board members, or our senior pastor. We compose our resignation letters, dream of how nice it would be to be to change churches, and speculate on how unjust it is that someone so wonderful could be stuck with such ungrateful people.

If we live in Florida or Southern California, chances are we may have never experienced SAD. One study showed that the farther north a person lives in North America, the greater the percentage of people who were *severely* affected.

- Florida—1.4 percent
- Maryland—6.3 percent
- New York—8.0 percent
- New Hampshire—10.0 percent

These percentages represent the severe cases. An equal percentage of SAD sufferers will experience only moderate symptoms. If we live in Baltimore, Chicago, or Denver, and we minister to 50 junior and senior high school students, about seven or eight will experience the significant emotional undertow of SAD. It's only a small number, but the destructive potential is real.

Knowing this, what should we do about SAD? Every November I tell the students and staff about SAD. I remind them that the feelings, if they come, are normal. I implore them not to drop out during this time but to intentionally be around people that can encourage them. Though I'm certainly no trained therapist, I observe that "sad" teenagers are generally over it by Christmas. "Sad" probably isn't SAD. But if a student is feeling down for weeks and months beyond, it could be clinical depression instead.[10] Personally, I have a policy to never, ever resign from *anything* in November. When I go to youth worker meetings, I try to watch for those who are feeling low and encourage them, if I can.

"THOSE ABOVE"

OTHER VOLUNTEERS

PARENTS

TEENAGERS

YOUTH WORK

YOU!

So if you're in the northern part of the United States, knowing about SAD can help—even though I know that sounds too simplistic.

Jim moved from San Diego to Portland due to a job change. He found a good church and volunteered in the youth ministry. He'd read about SAD and knew the Pacific Northwest was not exactly San Diego when it came to sunshine and temperature.

He arrived in Portland on July 1. Sure enough, in mid-November, he was feeling down and was sensing an emotional pull back toward San Diego. He knew he was SAD with a capital S. He put a big picture of the ocean up in his office, and he shared his feelings openly with the pastoral staff and other youth workers he saw frequently. He made it through his first winter, and now, three years later, he's an avid backpacker. He loves Portland and loves how close the mountains are. The ocean picture in his office has been replaced by one of Mount Hood.

The "Field" of Youth Work

If each of America's 330,000 Protestant and Roman Catholic churches has 1.5 people who work with young people in some way, then well over a half million of us in the country are engaged in the field of youth ministry. That's a lot of people! There are at least 100 Christian colleges/universities that offer an academic major in youth ministry. Many seminaries offer master's degrees in youth ministry, and there are a couple of youth ministry Ph.D. programs now available. With so many people involved in youth ministry, it makes sense that there is a lot of help and encouragement available to us as volunteers as we survey this "field."

YOUTH MINISTRY MAKES A DIFFERENCE

"THOSE ABOVE"

OTHER VOLUNTEERS

PARENTS

TEENAGERS

YOUTH WORK

YOU!

> *One of the top five things youth workers enjoy about volunteering: "Feeling that I'm contributing to our church and the kingdom by 'being there' for these kids."*
> *—Volunteer Youth Workers Survey*

We know we're helping our church by working with teenagers. And though we may not see results *this week* in a specific student, we get a chance to see, over time, positive impact from youth ministry. Last week at youth group, Brandon, one of our four student leaders, was very distracting to others during the serious portion of our youth group meeting. He wasn't doing anything criminal, just annoying. But I know that while he wasn't exactly a spiritual giant last week, the overall trajectory in his life is good and I'll have the privilege of watching him grow.

People with Ph.D.s have been studying youth and religion for a few decades now and have come up with data that has caused quite a stir in academia. What are the findings of this research that is gaining attention worldwide? Christian teenagers have assets their less religious peers do not have. An "asset" is the presence of something positive or the absence of something negative.

Statistically, Christian youth stay in school longer, are healthier, feel better about themselves, are more likely to volunteer their time to help others, and have better relationships with their parents. Christian youth also get sexually transmitted diseases less, get pregnant less, drink less, do drugs less, break the law less, and go to jail less than their not-as-religious peers.[11]

The term sociologists use for this is *religiosity*. Religiosity is measured by a person's prayer patterns, Bible reading, attitudes about God, church and youth group attendance, and any other expression of faith.

So here is the key, which now helps us as youth workers understand that we're doing something important not only for the kingdom but also for a civil society: Youth group participation is a part of this "youth religiosity" the academics are measuring. What students believe actually makes a difference in how they behave. What we do as volunteers helps teenagers have a faith that makes a difference.

Sometimes I actually remember this when, at the end of a long day at work, I'm at the grocery store buying cookies and apple/raspberry juice for youth group. I might rather be home taking a power nap, but I just remember, *youth ministry makes a difference*.

CHAPTER 8

PURPOSE, PURPOSE, PURPOSE

> *One of the top five most frustrating things for volunteer youth workers: "There are unclear expectations of what I'm supposed to be doing."*
> —Volunteer Youth Workers Survey

If you were to take a Christian college "Introduction to Youth Ministry" course just about anywhere in the country, you'd likely be introduced to a few connected notions. These notions answer the question, "What should I be doing as a youth worker, and why?"

1. A balanced youth ministry offers something for all teenagers, regardless where they are spiritually. Realize it's often not possible to reach all of their needs at the same gathering.

2. In the New Testament there are a couple of great models for this balanced approach to ministry. These models can apply regardless of setting: big church, small church, urban church, rural church, USA, or Slovenia. What are those models?

Then you'd go on to learn the gist of each of the models. Here they are:

"THOSE ABOVE"

OTHER VOLUNTEERS

PARENTS

TEENAGERS

YOUTH WORK

YOU!

The Win/Build/Equip/Unleash Model

This model anchors in the pattern of ministry of Jesus in the Gospels. Do a quick read of the Gospels yourself and see that Jesus did all of these things. Many youth groups focus on "winning" and "building"; they offer a weekly program with the purpose of helping Christian teenagers grow spiritually, while at the same time trying to keep unchurched youth interested in Christianity. Sunday school is an example of a program that usually has the specific purpose of building people spiritually. Along with building programs, youth groups often add activities that focus primarily on evangelism (winning) to attract more unchurched teenagers.

Many youth ministries are not so good at "equipping" and "unleashing"—that is, helping teenagers understand their strengths and gifts, and then giving them opportunities to use those strengths and gifts within the youth group, the church, and the community.

> *"Encourage the church group to clarify what they hope you to accomplish."*
> –Volunteer from urban Ontario

In the middle school group I lead (usually 10 youth plus two college-age volunteers), our normal Wednesday night gathering consists of hangout time (6:45-7:15), games (7:15-7:45), Bible time (highly interactive, not a speech or sermon—7:45-8:15), and snacks (8:15-8:30). About two-thirds of the teenagers who come are Christians, and the rest are these students' friends, none of whom are Christians. Once every four or five weeks we have "Service Project Ministry" night. This aims at the equipping/unleashing purposes. On Service Project Ministry night the students have two choices. They can bake cookies in the church kitchen to give (that evening) to the people coming out of a church prayer meeting. The cookies express thanks for their prayers for the church and for the youth group. We do more than teach students how to make cookies. We talk about why people gather to pray for the church and for personal prayer requests. We talk about why it means so much to an older person to be acknowledged by a teenager. We talk through the actual process of entering the room, choosing a person, approaching them, and thanking them.

The second choice is to go visit people from the church who have interesting stories to tell. In the van en route, we brainstorm questions they might ask and discuss why it means so much for an adult to see a teenager express interest in their lives.

No, neither of these ideas is on the same scale as going to Uganda to build orphanages, but for our little group and for these teenagers (many of whom lack financial resources), these two choices provide a way for them to "give back"...and they actually enjoy it. The more opportunities we give students to "try out" different ministries, the more able they will be to get a feel for their own giftedness, strengths, and calling. All of us on the volunteer staff are watching for moments when the students shine, and we affirm the good we see in them.

The Five Purposes Model
I suspect you've heard of Purpose Driven®. Rick Warren's book, *The Purpose Driven Church*[12] helped church leaders see that a balanced ministry should include each of the five things described in the book of Acts about the early church: worship, disicpleship, fellowship, outreach, and ministry. Following this book, Doug Fields wrote *Purpose Driven Youth Ministry*[13] to help youth groups contextualize

"THOSE ABOVE"

OTHER VOLUNTEERS

PARENTS

TEENAGERS

YOUTH WORK

YOU!

this approach. A key emphasis of this book is that each of our youth ministry "program components" should have a defined purpose. Many youth workers have found this idea very helpful and have organized their ministry something like this:

- Evangelism—Primarily aiming at the unchurched
- Worship—Helping Christian teenagers connect with God
- Fellowship—Christian teenagers become family, the body of Christ
- Ministry—Helping teenagers serve others
- Discipleship—Teaching for spiritual growth

There is tremendous variation around the country as to what youth groups actually do to make each of these five things happen, but the point is simple: The leaders, and even key students, know the purpose of each event or gathering of the youth group.

> "*Set clear expectations, work as a team, connect youth ministry to the larger parish as a part of a comprehensive plan.*"
> —Volunteer from suburban Delaware

Both the Win/Build and Five Purposes models help answer the question, "What should I be doing and why?" Anything and everything that happens in the youth ministry should fit into one or more aspects of these models. Too theoretical? Here are two examples.

I was the youth pastor in one church for 14 years. We had two major retreats each year for the senior high group—with dramatically different purposes. The volunteer staff, the elders, key youth, and even not-so-key youth all knew the purpose of these retreats.

The Summer Retreat Purpose: Fellowship/Spiritual Growth/Worship

We welcomed the incoming ninth-graders, had lots of fun stuff to build community, enjoyed small groups times, and participated in whole-group worship and teaching. Our own teenagers were *not* allowed to invite friends who were not already part of the church or youth group. Why? The purpose was to create family, unity, and growth in Christ, without distraction.

The Winter Retreat Purpose: Outreach

We urged students to invite their non-Christian friends. The whole-group gatherings (we called 'em "Club") were fun and funny, and the "talk" was aimed to be of particular interest to those not yet within the Christian faith. All of our own youth group knew this retreat was not going to include deep teaching or worship. They all knew that if they did not bring a friend, their job was still to come and be that welcoming, friendly, inclusive person for the friends brought by others.

Here's another example. Ever had a multi-church pudding fight? I've held several, actually. This is a BYOP (Bring Your Own Pudding) event. Each youth group makes and brings pudding, a flavor of their own choosing. Each youth group is assigned a "home base" in the church parking lot. Paper plates and cups are provided, and at the sound of "go" all heaven breaks loose.

If you should ever have your own pudding fight, here are two cautionary notes. First, make sure you have hoses running (held by an adult). Pudding stings when it gets in your eyes so it is important to have fresh water in abundance handy. Second and

"THOSE ABOVE"

OTHER VOLUNTEERS

PARENTS

TEENAGERS

YOUTH WORK

YOU!

critically important if you value your life, *never have a pudding fight in the church parking lot the day a wedding is being held at your church*. As valiantly as one tries to hose down said parking lot, it's impossible to get every last bit of pudding off that pavement. And know this: *There is no fury like that of the mother of the bride faced with a pudding-pocked parking lot.* (Can you guess I have personal experience in this?)

Now I can hear you ask, "What's the purpose of that mess, Len?!" Well, for us this was an outreach event...students invited friends. No, there was not a gospel presentation or "talk." It was just good (not so clean) fun. Teenagers invited friends, and their friends saw that we could have fun without being drunk or high. It made it easier for students to invite these same friends to our regular youth group meeting. The parents, church members, and leaders not only knew about these events but they also knew the purpose. The youth ministry program also did a lot as a group to raise money and awareness to help less fortunate persons, whether close by or far away.

GONE GLOBAL

"THOSE ABOVE"

OTHER VOLUNTEERS

PARENTS

TEENAGERS

YOUTH WORK

YOU!

All of us in youth ministry—full time, part time, or volunteer—are part of a global movement.

> "The local church is the hope of the world, and the youth will transform this world!"
>
> —Volunteer from suburban Colorado

There are youth pastors, youth ministry degree programs, and volunteer youth workers on every continent (except Antarctica). The joys and frustrations are similar everywhere. This was confirmed to me when I did an international youth workers survey a couple years ago. The top joys youth workers named were "seeing kids get it," "spending time with youth," and "worshipping with youth." These responses could have been from Kansas, California, or Tennessee, but they came from youth workers in Nigeria, Hong Kong, and Peru. These were not Americans doing youth ministry internationally; these were local youth workers, all with college youth ministry degrees or the equivalent. How about the frustrations of youth ministry? Youth workers named "kids dropping out of church after age 18," "church bureaucracy," and "lack of money." Those words came from New Zealand, the Netherlands, and South Africa.[14]

Among the many questions I asked in my international survey was "What programming does your youth group have for the purpose of spiritual growth?" Here is a snapshot of those results:

Percent of Respondents From Each Country/Continent Which Had this Program Component

	Africa	South Africa	Australia/New Zealand	India	Asia	Europe	United Kingdom	South America/ Central America	North America	Mean Percentage of All Responses
Weekly meeting	75	91	71	100	43	43	57	83	70	67
Sunday school	25	25	40	0	44	21	26	17	55	40
Small groups	33	50	68	25	53	43	69	17	66	60
Discipleship groups	25	25	43	25	75	7	35	67	34	40
Confirmation/ Catechism	8	25	18	0	0	42	39	9	24	21
Other	17	8	21	25	18	11	27	33	11	17

There were some surprises in this research. North American youth ministries include Sunday school as part of their approach to spiritual growth far more than youth ministries in the rest of the world. Also, I had assumed that virtually everyone everywhere had a weekly youth group meeting. Apparently not so! While 70 percent of survey respondents from North America reported a regular youth group meeting that included spiritual growth as a purpose, in Europe and Asia less than half the ministries did. What did they do instead? Later in the survey I learned that most of the "non-weekly meeting" ministries operated out of youth centers; facilities opened regularly after school or in the evening. I've seen some of these personally: storefront youth centers in Manila (Philippines), rehabbed unused church sanctuaries in Dundee (Scotland), and community rooms in high-rise apartment buildings in Hong Kong. The exciting thing is that we are all, in youth ministry worldwide, attempting to partner with students in their spiritual journey, figuring out together what it means to be a disciple of Jesus Christ.

"THOSE ABOVE"

OTHER VOLUNTEERS

PARENTS

TEENAGERS

YOUTH WORK

YOU!

THE WILDLIFE

Teenagers

This field guide now moves from the terrain to consider a certain kind of wildlife. Let's look at those wonderful (and sometimes frightening) creatures, the teenagers (and pre-teens) who inhabit the world of middle school (grades 6-8) and high school (grades 9-12). We will look at some of their characteristics and what it means to work with them as a volunteer.

THE CEREBRAL UPGRADE

"THOSE ABOVE"

OTHER VOLUNTEERS

PARENTS

TEENAGERS

YOUTH WORK

YOU!

Several years ago the church I now attend was larger. Our youth pastor was out of town. He asked me to lead the junior high group Wednesday night. Yikes! Nearly 40 students showed up, but miracle of miracles, the game time went well (translation: no teenagers were "too cool" to participate) and even the Bible talk went well. I took a wild risk and suggested we close in conversational prayer. We had been talking about how the early church was unified, supportive of each other, and really focused on Jesus and serving one another. I suggested we thank God for what he had given us as a youth group.

Shock! About half the students actually prayed verbal, sincere prayers of thanks and spiritual hope. I thought, "Lord, you can take me home now; it doesn't get much better than this!" I closed the session in a brief prayer. After the "Amen" I stood there, just savoring the moment. The boys were sitting in a semi-circle to my left. The girls, same thing on the right, facing the boys.

Tom shouted out, "Hey Liz, you're fat, and you're ugly!"

Liz jumped to her feet, burst into tears, and ran from the room followed by three of her friends. The boys, every one of them, laughed uproariously, giving each other high fives, some rolling in laughter at such an incredibly perfectly timed insult. The girls stared at these boys in utter disgust, anger, and disbelief.

And with that, our happy youth group Bible study was over... students went out to the parking lot for their awaiting rides home. I could just imagine what was being said.

What would you have done? Called an elders meeting? Ban Tom from the group for two months—or years?

What did I do? I found Tom in the parking lot. "Tom, what you said in there was wrong. Weren't you one of the guys who had just prayed, 'Lord, thank you for our great youth group'?"

Tom looked at me, no repentance on his face. "She's my sister; I can say what I want!" Apparently, in Tom's pre-cerebral upgraded mind, there was no connection between being a Christian and being nice to a sibling sister.

I left it at that. I knew there would come a day, probably sooner than later, that Tom would mature to the point where he realize that stuff we talked about in youth group also applied at home. His cerebral upgrade, I assumed, would happen and that would take care of it.

In the brain of a teenager, something truly amazing happens in adolescence. More mental wires get made and connected. Previously unused brain capacity arouses itself into life. A child's mind changes, often within a period of only a few months, into an entirely different organ. This cerebral upgrade starts occurring in girls first, during ages 11 to 14. Most boys, for reasons known only to God, don't get the upgrade until after age 15. Specifically, early adolescent boys may have a pre-frontal cortex, but it is not plugged in yet. The lights may be on, but no one is home. The pre-frontal cortex is the area of the brain from which risk assessment, ability to think about the future and make plans accordingly, and abstract thinking arise. Most girls have this by age 12. Most boys don't have it yet at age 14.

> **"Seeing the lights come on when they finally understand some aspect of their faith that was previously just some piece of info they had to memorize but didn't fully grasp is the most rewarding part."**
> *–Volunteer from suburban California*

Teenagers who are getting upgraded or have already had it happen can make faith more than just a hand-me-down from their parents. They can reason and understand why Jesus died for them. They can understand the gospel at a whole new level and embrace it themselves. The process may be messy with questions: Why should I believe in God? Why isn't Islam as good as or better than Christianity? How can something that happened so long ago make a difference today? If our teenagers are asking these questions, that's a good sign!

When it comes to self-esteem, most seventh-graders won't feel secure unless they have material things or abilities that their peers admire. Later, though, they'll understand who they are in Christ and the true foundation and comfort this brings.

When we understand these things as youth workers, we don't have to go to bed at night wondering why the boys don't "get it." Most will, in time. When it comes to teen behavior, understanding the cerebral

"THOSE ABOVE"

OTHER VOLUNTEERS

PARENTS

"TEENAGERS"

YOUTH WORK

YOU!

upgrade makes a bit more sympathetic toward young males who act out. The part of their brain that sees themselves and assesses risk is, quite literally, not plugged in yet. Of course, we as youth workers must be clear about behavioral expectations and provide clear and meaningful consequences for non-cooperation (such as a time-out if a guy doesn't settle down when appropriate).

CHAPTER 11

AGE-APPROPRIATE BEHAVIOR

If you are over 30 and you aren't a schoolteacher, parent of teenagers, or a student of adolescent culture, just the thought of being with teenagers can be daunting. We gain valuable insight into youth behavior from understanding the "cerebral upgrade," but that's not the whole story.

It is easy for adults to forget, or at least not appreciate, the power of the social dynamics among youth. I see the power of this every week.

Friendships

When contemplating their potential attendance at a youth group meeting or special event, the main question is not "What are we going to do?" The main question is "Who's going to be there?" I try to harness the power of friendships in a couple of ways. When we have small groups as part of our youth meeting, I make sure students are with their friends. When we play some kind of game or sport that requires teams, I *never* "count off." Especially with young students, announcing we're going to count off for teams means some will quickly rearrange themselves to ensure they'll be on the same team.

So how to "pick" teams? I just say, "We're going to need four teams for this game. Everyone stand up and make sure you are with one or two other people you enjoy being around." I then walk among the

"THOSE ABOVE"

OTHER VOLUNTEERS

PARENTS

TEENAGERS

YOUTH WORK

YOU!

groups and say, "OK, you three over there, you two over there, you four go that way…" until things are basically balanced. If things need to be evened up, and if I'm in a youth group that has a student leadership team, I might say, "OK, Mike, you need to move over to that team, and Kaira, you need to switch over here." The student leaders know this might happen and have agreed to it as part of what it means to be in leadership.

In short, we'll sleep better at night as volunteer youth workers when we understand the high importance of friendships among youth.

> "Enjoy every moment you can with these kids. Always be careful not to judge the kids. Many of the kids have no guidance and may be labeled as a 'troublemaker' because they are seeking attention and this is the only way to get it."
>
> –Volunteer from urban Indiana

Guy/girl relationships

In youth work we get to watch an amazing transition take place. It is not hard to see these stages on the elementary school playground, the middle school lunch room, or the high school youth group.

Ages 8-11: "Boy Germs, Girl Germs!" Virtually no male/female interaction or friendships with peers.

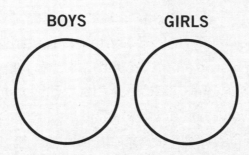

Ages 12-15: Some male/female friendships forming among those who are most social (and often the most physically developed).

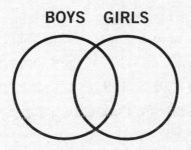

Ages 16-18: Many if not most youth are OK with and have male/female friendships and interaction.

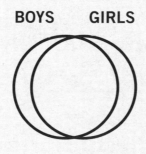

"THOSE ABOVE"

OTHER VOLUNTEERS

PARENTS

"TEENAGERS"

YOUTH WORK

YOU!

One evening a couple of years ago, I was sitting outside the circle of about 20 middle school youth at our normal weekly meeting. Another volunteer was leading the Bible discussion. About halfway through, Carli, a 12-year-old girl, turned to me and whispered with a huge smile and dreamy look on her face, "Jordan is *so cute*!" My response? Well, it wasn't "Turn around; you should be listening to Marv's great Bible teaching!" Rather I leaned over and whispered back, "I'm not a very good judge of male cuteness, but I'm glad you are, Carli." She smiled even larger and returned to face toward the circle and her ardent, dreamy gaze at Jordan.

During our youth group hangout time before the meeting starts, I have the fun of watching tentative steps toward male/female interaction and friendship happen. A few weeks ago Anthony was chasing Laura, throwing at her with all his might the (very soft and squishy) stuffed animals we have around for various sports-related purposes. A week or two later I noticed Laura chasing Anthony, armed with the same stuffed animal projectiles. Last week they were throwing the Frisbee® back and forth *together*. As an adult, don't miss the joy of these moments. I can imagine Anthony laying in bed that night, maybe his heart racing, and the incredible achievement of playing Frisbee® (alone!) with Laura. I could see written all over Laura's smiling face that she would talk late into the night with her sister about the momentous nature of what had occurred. They would certainly talk about what might come next: texting? an actual phone call?

DISCIPLINE

"THOSE ABOVE"

OTHER VOLUNTEERS

PARENTS

TEENAGERS

YOUTH WORK

YOU!

> *One of the top five most frustrating things about volunteering in youth ministry: "Unruly kids ruin it for me."*
> *—Volunteer Youth Workers Survey*

Are the teenagers in your youth group perfect angels? Mine aren't. Most of the "issues" are minor, such as not settling down when we have our Bible time in our youth group meeting or chasing each other with wet paper towels from the kitchen or bathroom.

For minor problems, I find just a gentle reminder is all it takes. "Hey, we just had a great time playing games so now it's time to settle down. If you can't handle that tonight, you can go home if you wish—no problem." Or, "Our poor janitor will have a heart attack if we have a water war inside the church building. Here, throw these stuffed animals instead."

In the last six months I've only had to eject two students from the group, not allowing them to return for two months. The infraction? Throwing hard objects at the heads of the others and denying (repeatedly) that they were doing so, even when seen (multiple times) by myself and the other staff. I think we owe it to the parents that youth group be a safe place, quite literally.

> ## "Out-of-control kids make it so difficult. I love working with teens, but sometimes I wonder if they hear the gospel message when things are so chaotic."
> —Volunteer from suburban Missouri

Clear expectations

We owe it to both youth and parents to be clear about behavior expectations. I try to keep it simple. For example...

At regular youth group events (including the weekly meeting):
1. If you come, you stay until the end. (That is, no coming, then disappearing, only to reappear at the end.)
2. When we're done with games, everyone relinquishes their cell phones until the end of the meeting.
3. Can't settle down when appropriate? Sent home after two reminders.

At a retreat or special event:
1. Cooperate with the leadership of the event.
2. Attend all meetings of the retreat.
3. No controlled substances allowed.

Every group is different, of course, and issues vary by size and composition of the group. In larger groups I've worked with, we've had other stated expectations. This is has been especially important if the group has a high percentage of teenagers who are not from church families. Extra stated expectations (with the junior high group) include no swearing, no bullying, and a reminder to respect the church property.

"I was a little confused when…"
One way to approach a teenager whose behavior needs correcting is to invite conversation, rather than making an accusation. I find it doesn't invite immediate rejection and does indeed open the door to conversation, especially when followed with "help me understand what's going on." Here are some actual examples:

> *"Unruly kids are the primary source of my frustration. Their lack of ability to discipline themselves to be attentive makes it impossible to minister to them. They just aren't listening."*
> —Volunteer from urban Oklahoma

Situation: A guy continually makes life miserable for one of the girls in the group.

Me: *I'm a little confused, Jason, when I see you bullying Lydia. In each of the last three weeks I've seen you mocking her and saying horrible things about her in front of others. Help me understand what's going on.*

"THOSE ABOVE"

OTHER VOLUNTEERS

PARENTS

TEENAGERS

YOUTH WORK

YOU!

Jason: (Walked away without saying a word. But he never was a bully to her again!)

Situation: A teenager from a non-church family is distracting and disrupting during the serious portion of our youth group meeting. I speak with Brandon prior to the start of our next meeting.

Me: *Say, Brandon, I'm a little confused about something. You're here nearly every week and you seem to like coming, but when we have our time talking about the Bible, you seem like you want to ruin it for the ones who are really interested. Help me understand what's going on.*

Brandon: *I don't know; it's hard to sit still.*

Me: *I notice you really focus when one of your friends is up front, leading part of the Bible study, and that's really cool. I'd like you to be the one "up front" some of the time at next week's meeting, and here's what I have in mind..."*

Brandon led the Book section the next week (see Chapter 14's discussion of Hook Book Look Took). He did a fine job and was much cooperative and focused—though not perfectly—in the weeks that followed.

> *"Don't take their 'rejection' personally. Sometimes it takes awhile for them to trust you and return your friendship. Don't be afraid of the kids that seem really hard or worldly. They are usually the ones that just want to know if you really care."*
> —Volunteer from suburban Iowa

When all else fails

Sometimes our best efforts at loving care and discipline still don't work. I've seen situations where teenagers stop coming because the behavior of others is so obnoxious and disruptive. If our best efforts don't produce behavior change in disruptive students or if the purpose of the group is being thwarted, it is sad but OK to tell students they are no longer allowed to attend. It is easy to feel guilty about such a decision or feel like we've failed. But this difficult decision can yield healthy results for everyone involved.

"THOSE ABOVE"

OTHER VOLUNTEERS

PARENTS

TEENAGERS

YOUTH WORK

YOU!

CHAPTER 13

WHAT NEUROSCIENCE IS TELLING US ABOUT WHY SOME KIDS SEEM SO MESSED UP

"THOSE ABOVE"

OTHER VOLUNTEERS

PARENTS

TEENAGERS

YOUTH WORK

YOU!

> *One of the top five most frustrating things about volunteering in youth ministry: "Unruly kids ruin it for me."*
>
> *–Volunteer Youth Workers Survey*

If you are discouraged or frustrated by teenagers who consistently act up or act out, this will give perspective on your predicament.

Talaris Research Institute of Seattle is one of the many academic centers with a focus on brain research, especially related to children and youth. The institute's founding director, Dr. John Medina, has come up with 12 brain principles, or research-related facts that he calls Brain Rules.[15] In particular, Brain Rule 8 can have an impact on our experience as volunteer youth workers. Here it is:

Stressed brains don't learn the same way.

What Medina and others are finding is that emotional tension and trauma experienced in the first couple of years of a child's life have significant negative effects on brain development. What do they mean by "tension and trauma"? Significant marital conflict that creates a negative emotional environment is a qualifier. Verbal or physical abuse qualifies. Lack of caring adult support qualifies.

> *"The only frustration I deal with is how to effectively impact kids who have no concept of authority, authority figures, personal discipline (how to sit down and be quiet or follow the directions of the leaders), or concept of right and wrong. My frustration stems from knowing that we (the youth ministry team–a phenomenal team) are the only influence for even decent, normal, socially acceptable life, not to mention the only touch of God."*
>
> *–Volunteer from urban Oklahoma*

An extreme example of Brain Rule 8 comes from the work of Megan Gunner in Canada. You may recall that under communism in Romania, the country became infamous for what some in the U.S. called "Romanian pediatric concentration camps," otherwise known as orphanages. Children received virtually no loving care or touch; they were just fed, changed, and otherwise ignored.

Her study of 110 Canadian families who adopted Romanian children showed these adoptees fall into two distinct groups. In the first group, the children, now ages 10-14, are normal, happy, Canadian children. Gunner calls the second group, however, "The Titanic

Group." She explains, "It is like *they hit something*." These children are ill tempered, oft out of control, and do very poorly in school.

Why the difference between the two groups? The now happy group's children were all adopted before they were 4 months old. According to Gunner, after children are 4 months old, it is too late for any amount of love, care, or good parenting to compensate for the deprivation or trauma experienced earlier. My heart goes out to those loving and generous Canadian parents who reached out to these children, not knowing they were adopting orphans with such deep emotional issues.

While Gunner's research is narrowly focused on these Romanian adoptees, the research consensus from dozens of other studies is very simply this: If the very early months and years of a child's life are lacking in care or contain an environment of emotional toxicity, brain development is negatively affected. This negative effect will likely show up in both childhood and adolescence, in one or more of the following traits:

- decreased attention span
- less able to self-soothe
- longer recovery time from life's stressors
- less impulse control
- more behavioral problems
- psychiatric disorders
- less ability to build close relationships

Sound like any teenagers you know?

As a volunteer in youth ministry, this impacts my thinking and actions in two ways.

"THOSE ABOVE"

OTHER VOLUNTEERS

PARENTS

TEENAGERS

YOUTH WORK

YOU!

First, it makes me more compassionate and grace giving to students who consistently exhibit one or more of these behaviors. For example, when Andrew came to youth group the first time, as a sixth-grader, he seemed sullen and withdrawn. Not very unusual for an 11-year-old boy. As the weeks went by, he became "comfortable" enough to bully some of the other students. He seemed angry often. I was correcting him over some misbehavior one evening and he looked at me with hatred in his eyes and exclaimed, "I just want to be Satan! I just want to kill people!!!" He came to youth group regularly the next two and a half years; we had to eject him several times for extreme or threatening behavior. One of the things that helped us adults "hang in there" with Andrew is that we became aware of his home life and early background. To say his early childhood was "filled with toxicity" really does not do justice to how bad it was for him. (By the way, he is maturing, is in high school now, and, as far as I know, he no longer aspires to be Satan.)

> *"Our ministry consists of children and teens with developmental, physical, emotional, and mental health issues. We have been threatened with guns and hurt by teens who come. The children as young as 8 years old steal from us and others and have no comprehension that it is wrong. Along with the language— again, they don't know they are swearing. It can be frustrating at times. Also, we deal with unwed mothers."*
> —Volunteer from rural New York

Secondly, I do everything I can to support and build healthy marriages. There are so many good resources to help couples. My students at Nyack College often hear me talk about the ingredients to good male/female relationships.[16] As of this writing my wife and I have been married roughly 13,500 days (we have a big party every 1,000 days) so I guess we can speak with some experience, having worked through, over the decades, a host of very significant issues in our relationship.

"THOSE ABOVE"

OTHER VOLUNTEERS

PARENTS

TEENAGERS

YOUTH WORK

YOU!

THE JOY OF TEACHING YOUTH PART 1

"THOSE ABOVE"

OTHER VOLUNTEERS

PARENTS

TEENAGERS

YOUTH WORK

YOU!

> ### One of the top five joys of youth ministry volunteering: "Being able to teach."
> #### –Volunteer Youth Workers Survey

If we think of what we're doing with teenagers as not just youth work but youth ministry, it implies we have a spiritual purpose. Despite what some may think, youth ministry is *not* babysitting. Teaching is one of the key distinctions that helps distinguish youth ministry as having a spiritual purpose beyond just social connection.

I suggest two important principles when it comes to teaching teenagers:

1. **Yes, we should teach.**
   We teach with our lives. When students see how we react to setbacks, disappointments, or confusion, we're teaching them a great deal. I received an e-mail recently from a girl who was in my youth group 25 years ago (no kidding). "I really wanted to thank you for all those hikes and backpacking trips...I learned so much from you, just watching you relate to everyone and how you dealt with bad weather and problems...Thank you for your

example in Scripture memory…and I still remember some of the psalms we memorized on those trips together."

Jesus had three years of hangout time with his disciples, and they learned a lot by just watching him, but Jesus also taught with words. If you've seen a "Red Letter" edition of the New Testament, where all of Jesus' words are printed in red, it becomes obvious that he said and taught a great deal.

If you are a volunteer and someone else is the teaching-speaking person, you have the luxury of focusing on teaching-by-life. Your focus is to know, care about, pray for, encourage, and love the teenagers around you. You also speak truth through your words, but you don't have to craft that into a message for an entire group at once. But if you are the teacher-speaker, what then? This takes us to our second principle.

2. **Real teaching cultivates life change. If students are not changing in their outlook and actions or seem bored and stop listening, then you are not actually teaching.**

Think back to your time in school. Were you ever bored to tears in some classes, yet really engaged in and excited about others? Have you ever sat through a sermon (or hundreds of them) that just seemed dry and lifeless? Have you ever watched someone speak or teach in youth group and it was obvious the students were not interested? Have you been in a youth group where there seemed to be no any visible evidence of spiritual growth?

In most youth groups around the country, someone gives a talk. The presentation itself may be only a few minutes or as long as 30. It may be supported with YouTube® or movie clips, PowerPoint®, or other media and presentation support.

There are many ways to teach the Bible and spiritual things, and certainly a "youth talk" can be used of God to produce good in teenagers—especially if it is followed by discussion in small groups about specific application and accountability.[17] My observation is that while "the youth talk" may be OK, there are better ways to engage the hearts and minds of students in a teaching situation. Here is my favorite.

Hook Book Look Took

A few weeks ago during our Bible time, I had our students (middle schoolers; 11 present that night) gather around a big square table. Much to their surprise (and delight) I dumped in the middle of the table a huge box of Thomas the Train® items, which included cars, signs, other traffic related paraphernalia, and a few barnyard animals. (Shhh. Don't tell anyone: I raided the preschool storage room for this treasure—and yes, I did put it all back when we were done!)

Next, I told them, "Use these pieces to create a traffic scenario that includes conflict." Wow, it was like I'd given them each $100. They immediately, and with great delight, constructed their scenarios. After a few minutes, each one, around the table, explained their scenario while they moved their train and other pieces accordingly. Some were short and simple explanations—cow on truck, crosses tracks, truck stalls, train sees it, and stops just in time, but the engineer is really mad at the driver. Other stories were, shall we say, considerably more detailed:

"Well, there was a terrorist plot that was foiled just in the nick of time by the feds in a nearby city, but the bad guys managed to get away into the countryside and they hopped a slow-moving train. The engineer could have seen them hop on in his rearview mirror, but he

"THOSE ABOVE"

OTHER VOLUNTEERS

PARENTS

TEENAGERS

YOUTH WORK

YOU!

was texting his girlfriend, who lived in the town ahead. The terrorists slowly made their way toward the front of the train, thinking they would hijack it when suddenly two SWAT team helicopters appeared, and a machine-gun battle took place. Two cows were killed nearby during the fight, and meanwhile, the girlfriend was watching Oprah when suddenly..."

All of us around the table either were laughing so hard our stomachs hurt or were sitting in wide-eyed, drop-jaw amazement as this story unfolded. When I finally was able to compose myself, I said, "As you know, we've been looking at a letter that Paul wrote to the Christians in a town about the size of ours, called Philippi. Paul wanted those Christians to be the kind of people that learned how to have less conflict and fewer problems with others."

I read from Philippians 4:8-9 and followed the reading with a few thoughts about why it might have been hard for the Philippian believers to think well of others: rich/poor, different ethnic backgrounds, different jobs, that sort of thing. I often ask a student to prepare in advance and lead the "read the passage and explain it" section.

Next I asked, "So, at school, or at home, or even here in youth group, what would be some examples of things people say about others that are put-downs?" The students found it easy to think of and mention different examples.

I handed out 3x5 cards and pencils. "Write down the initials of the person you have the most conflict with—the person you find it hardest to think or say good things about. We all agree that Jesus loves this person as much as he loves you, right? Now write down a couple of good things about them. This next week, I'd like you to keep this card where you'll see it as a reminder to pray for this person and for your own attitude."

To conclude, we lit a candle and turned out the lights, and I asked them to go around the table and each pray, thanking Jesus for his love for us and for his love for even the people we find it hard to get along with. Of the 11 present, only two passed; the rest prayed.

In this lesson, the Hook Book Look Took breakdown went like this:

Hook: An introduction with the purpose of getting everyone in the room focused on the same thing. I had our group create conflict scenarios with Thomas the Train® toys.

The end of the Hook is a bridge statement to the next section; in this case, the bridge statement was: "As you know, we've been looking at a letter that Paul wrote to the Christians in a town about the size of ours, called Philippi. Paul wanted these Christians to be the kind of people that learned how to have less conflict and fewer problems with others."

> *"It's wonderful to see God working in the lives of young people. It's wonderful to see their open hearts and be able to show them how to find God and serve the church and watch them get excited about it all."*
>
> *–Volunteer from suburban Maryland*

"THOSE ABOVE"

OTHER VOLUNTEERS

PARENTS

TEENAGERS

YOUTH WORK

YOU!

Book: The purpose of this section is to read and understand a Bible text, exploring what it meant to the people who heard or experienced it first. I read the Philippians passage and spoke about it briefly. Most of the time I have a student do this section. And yes, junior high students are quite capable of this. I ask the student a week ahead of time and call during the week to talk it though with him or her.

Look: This section is focused on trying to help students see how they fit into this picture—how the Scripture connects to today's world. It is important to let students talk...and if they are too shy to talk in front of the whole group, have them form pairs or small groups. We often break into guys-only, girls-only groups for this. In this example, I asked them to speak about specific examples from school, home, or church of people saying negative things.

Took: The key to this section is to let students think about how the Scripture might apply specifically to their situation. The students wrote down the person they're having the most trouble getting along with and then also jotted down two good things about them. I usually have something (in this case a 3x5 card) they take home with them. We lit the candle, turned down the lights, and prayed that we would be more able to get along with the person we'd chosen.

With a little practice, this method of teaching can become natural. Lawrence Richards introduced this method back in the 1970s in his book *Creative Bible Teaching*. Many youth ministry curriculum series, student Bible studies, and youth talk resources follow this format, using different verbiage for the Hook, Book, Look, and Took sections. Looking for resources?[18]

This method has several positive things about it:

1. **Variety.** The students really have no idea, week to week, what's going to happen. It is definitely not "same old, same old" when it comes to the Bible time.

> *"Teenagers amaze me all the time. I love when one remembers something from months ago or shares an insight that they've learned. I love to see them working with younger students and growing in ways they don't even see yet."*
>
> *—Volunteer from suburban Missouri*

2. **Interactivity.** In a 20- to 30-minute Bible time, I usually talk less than seven minutes. The entire remainder of the time is students talking or working on something.

3. **Involvement.** This approach is a good way to get students involved *actually leading*. When I first suggested the idea that teenagers could lead the Book section, both the students and adult leaders were shocked! After awhile, most students were happy to take a turn. This also gives me an excuse to contact the teenager during the week and process with them what they want to share about the passage. Involving students also forces me to be prepared one week in advance, so I can contact students about their part the next week.

"THOSE ABOVE"

OTHER VOLUNTEERS

PARENTS

TEENAGERS

YOUTH WORK

YOU!

4. **Transformation.** Most importantly, this approach focuses on connecting the Bible to real life, encouraging actual, specific, and measurable change.

Hook Book Look Took also works when large and small groups are used in the same meeting. For example, the Hook and Book with a little bit of the Look could be used with the whole group. The rest of the Look as well as the Took could then be done in small groups. It is especially powerful when the small groups are the same every week with the same adult or student leaders. Then, especially in high school, one can introduce accountability. "So next week, we're going to go around the circle. That person you wrote down that you have a lot of conflict with—next week we want to hear how it went. Let's agree to pray for each other daily, as this is going to be a hard one for some of us."

THE JOY OF TEACHING YOUTH PART 2

"THOSE ABOVE"

OTHER VOLUNTEERS

PARENTS

TEENAGERS

YOUTH WORK

YOU!

No matter what style or method we use in teaching, it will be even more effective if we are able to remember something called the "Seven Laws."

Howard Hendricks of Dallas Theological Seminary has a heart to help those ministering to children, youth, or adults in teaching and speaking situations. His "Seven Laws of the Teacher" are especially helpful to those of us who teach youth or adults.[19]

The Law of the Teacher: *"If you stop growing today, you should stop teaching tomorrow."*
If we as teachers are growing, our students can sense it. Is our life expanding or contracting? Are we learning new things, having new experiences? Are our examples when we speak or teach always from what happened years ago? If so, what might this convey to our students? You might be only 25, but you can seem *really ancient* to a 14-year-old if you've stopped growing. Are you reading? listening to podcasts? blogging about things in your life? learning new skills? trying things that put you in the position of a learner?

I realize any example I write here may seem ancient in just a year, but here it goes.

In late 2010 and early 2011, I used "Angry Birds" twice as an illustration in giving youth talks or Bible studies. Unfamiliar with

"Angry Birds"? At the time of this writing, it was the No. 1 paid download application for iPhones and iPads in over 60 countries (including the U.S., Canada, Russia, U.K., Germany, Pakistan, almost all of South America, plus Slovakia, Vietnam, Saudi Arabia, Hong Kong, and Latvia). "Angry Birds" is a great illustration of both seeking revenge and going on a quest. Both of these topics come up repeatedly in Scripture, as well as on TV and in movies.

I plan to use a travel experience from summer 2010 as an illustration soon. Did you know the canals in Amsterdam have to routinely be dredged because they get full of bicycles? No kidding. Saw it myself: a big barge, with a big crane with a big claw taking huge bites full of bikes out of a canal. I found out this is a *normal sight!* I'll let you wonder why (or let you visit ask.com), but it is a funny and good example of the "things below the surface eventually have to be dealt with."

> *"Kids aren't as scary as you think. Junior high kids want to learn more and get deeper in love with Jesus. They just need a little help focusing."*
> —Volunteer from suburban Alabama

The Law of Education: *"The true teacher is a coach, facilitator, and motivator, not just a lecturer."*
Effective teachers help students feel they are not being talked down to—that you and I are next to the students, along with them in the journey, not above them. I often think of the idea that "the ground is level at the foot of the cross." I'm trying to figure out how to daily live a Christian life, how to be a disciple, and how to authentically

represent Jesus with others who don't yet know him. My 11-, 12-, and 13-year-old youth group members are all dealing with one or more of these things as well; we are all learning together. Yes, I may know more and have more life experiences, but I'm still trying to figure things out. It is a lifelong journey. In a sense, then, I'm inviting them on this spiritual journey. A journey implies movement, and teaching for life change is about movement from point A to point B to point C and so on.

The Law of Communication: *"We must build bridges of common ground with those we wish to teach."*
Typically, we begin building a bridge of common ground in the Hook section of our teaching (see Chapter 14). We don't assume that every one of our students comes to youth group for the primary purpose of learning about Samuel's call from God, Paul's problem with misbehaving Corinthian Christians, or Jesus' view of religious snobs. All those topics are good, but no teenager lies awake at night in anticipation of our teaching about it at youth group.

Occasionally I meet a youth worker who is so convinced he is a great teacher and all he has to do is open his mouth and teenagers will listen with rapt attention. It seems that the person is really saying, "Hey, this is about me, my giftedness, and if you don't enjoy coming to watch me do what I think I'm good at, don't bother coming." Teaching becomes about them and not about students.

A quick look at the Gospels clearly reveals that Jesus was all about connecting with people. He was always building bridges, talking first about things that were common knowledge: figs, sheep, water, bread, farming. *He built a bridge first*, and the kingdom connection followed.

"THOSE ABOVE"

OTHER VOLUNTEERS

PARENTS

TEENAGERS

YOUTH WORK

YOU!

The Law of the Heart: *"We need to show it matters to us."*
The best way to show that our teaching matters to us personally is to share a personal illustration. Describe a struggle or experience related to the topic. Think of the range of human experience that comes up in Scripture, your own life, and the lives of your students: anticipation, disappointment, anger, hope, revenge, greed, sorrow, embarrassment, regret, surprise—it is all there and more. If we never share personal stories or illustrations, it may convey, "I am above you, better than you."

I'm five decades older than the 11-year-olds in my youth group, but I still remember the embarrassment and nervousness of my first weeks of middle school and high school. I sometimes give those terrible moments as illustrations. Pain, embarrassment, and nervousness are still a part of my experience even now. If a passage or topic is speaking or comforting to my personal situation, *it shows heart to share my experience*.

Of course, we must be discerning about what and how much we share. Can't stand your senior pastor? Probably not a good idea to share with the youth group! Are you battling lustful or greedy or angry thoughts? That is for your counselor, accountability partner, or your small group to hear about and pray for, not youth group.

Some youth workers try to show heart by screaming and yelling. There are some cultures and settings, I suppose, where "high volume" is considered normal and good. When I'm listening to a "screamer," I think about the students in the room. How many are thinking about how their mother or father or stepparent screams at them? Personally I don't think screaming at students is ever justified.

> *"I feel as though I don't know as much as I should to teach others. Teenagers can be hard to deal with, and I am a no-nonsense type person, so sometimes it can be a struggle."*
> *–Volunteer from suburban Virginia*

"THOSE ABOVE"

OTHER VOLUNTEERS

PARENTS

TEENAGERS

YOUTH WORK

YOU!

The Law of Encouragement: *"Look for ways to motivate."*

The best way to motivate your students toward learning is to affirm the group and individuals. Jesus spoke many words of encouragement and love to his disciples. For example, as the end neared for Jesus' time on earth, he spoke deeply and tenderly to the disciples. *"Now you are my friends, since I have told you everything the Father told me. You didn't choose me. I chose you. I appointed you to go and produce lasting fruit" (John 15:15-16).* Wow! All of the disciples could recall healings and all kinds of miracles (including weather management) and now he calls them his friends and chosen ones. That would make my day!

Look for ways to tell a student she really made a great comment or asked a great question. Thank another for his prayer or for helping plan something. Simple words, simple acts to show we care and appreciate—they all serve as encouragers.

The Law of Activity: *"Do some."*

It might be skits, creative worksheets, charades to guess Bible stories, or hip-hop lyrics for Psalm 23—whatever it is, if it is relevant to the main idea of the lesson, it will help students stay engaged. I use the law of activity even when I teach adults. Recently when I was teaching a group of about 40 adults sitting at round tables, my Hook was a *Jeopardy!*-type game on the theme of famous names. (Question: Many flashy NYC buildings bear this man's name. Answer: Who is Donald Trump?) I had a bag full of snack prizes. Each time a table won, they were tossed an edible prize. The prizes included a bag of pork rinds, salt and vinegar pretzels, and some other crazy things. The adults thought these were hilarious and seemed to really enjoy this opener.

Next I said, "The Old Testament is full of famous names. In the next two minutes, without looking at your Bible, see how many things you can come up with that Samuel is famous for."

Two minutes later, each table shared responses (no prizes this time). Then I used this bridge to the Book: "Today we're going to begin a series on the book of 1 Samuel. We can't cover the whole book in four sessions, but we'll focus on the important points in the first few chapters. Today we're going to look at God's call on Samuel's life and consider what God's call on our own lives might look like."

The Law of Readiness: *"If students are ready at the beginning, we can go even further in teaching."*
I focus on this law primarily when I do small group discipleship experiences. Recently I asked seven teenagers to meet for 10 weekly sessions of two hours each. They were also were asked to do projects between meetings. Since this was communicated as a specific and intense study for highly motivated students, our Hook each week is students reporting about their projects. Right after this time of sharing, we're ready to dive into the lesson.

In our typical weekly youth group meeting, I don't worry about this particular law. When I teach adults and it is a series of lessons, I usually ask three different adults each week to be on the lookout for the theme of our next lesson—in the New York Times, in movies, on TV, or in their readings. Though it may not seem like it, Bible themes pop up all the time in the media: commitment, revenge, shame, hope, disappointment, danger, stress, comfort. It is all there, every single week. You only have to be looking for it.

"THOSE ABOVE"

OTHER VOLUNTEERS

PARENTS

TEENAGERS

YOUTH WORK

YOU!

CHAPTER 16

THE JOY OF TEACHING YOUTH PART 3

"THOSE ABOVE"

OTHER VOLUNTEERS

PARENTS

TEENAGERS

YOUTH WORK

YOU!

Most of us love to teach in the same way we like to learn. This creates a problem: If we only teach the way that seems best and optimal to us, some of those we are teaching aren't "getting it" as easily as we might think; they may connect much better with a different learning style. Though many long academic books are dedicated to this subject, the basic idea is very simple: Most of us fall into one of four main learning styles.

- **Analytic:** These learners love systematic information, they love to take notes, they love lots of content, and they love to sit and listen. They like to know what to expect when in a learning situation.

- **Relational:** They don't know what they are learning until they can talk about it with others; the concept emerges and gains clarity as it is processed with and through others verbally.

- **Dynamic:** Here we have a group that really tunes in when things are creatively done. They love visual stimuli; they love to be surprised by what happens in a teaching/learning situation. And if they get to stand up, move around, or do something with their hands during a teaching/learning situation, well, it makes them happy and motivated.

- **Common Sense:** These may not say it out loud, but in their heads about every three minutes they are asking, "So what?" They love learning that is practical and immediately applicable to the situation at hand.

Be aware that while we may personally love hearing a good lecture and learning from it, the vast majority of teenagers (and young to middle-age adults, for that matter) do not find lectures to be the best way to learn. They learn much better with more participatory and active teaching methods, rather than just "sit and listen." This is well illustrated when some of our teenagers attend a university after high school graduation. What learning and teaching style do their professors have? Analytic. Teaching at the university level generally requires a Ph.D. This academic pursuit is generally a solitary quest: lots of note-taking and massive amounts of listening to lectures (scintillating or otherwise). It is *analytic-learner heaven.* The problem, however, is that only about 30 percent of college students are analytic learners.[20] Yes, non-analytic learners can learn from lectures; it is just they learn better in other ways.

Glancing at the Hook Book Look Took format for teaching (see Chapter 14), you can see that this particular method of teaching can hit all four learning styles in a single session.

The Hook is a great place to engage dynamic learners.

The Book is ideal for analytic learners.

The Look can make relational learners so happy.

The Took is the natural place for common sense learners to really tune in.

> "We hang out with our kids. We love them, they love us, and they love each other. We have fun and play a lot! But I am not convinced we are giving them the foundation they need to hang on to their faith for a lifetime, especially as they go off to college. I think we give them milk when we could be having steak when we are together. They are so capable of handling the deep truths of the faith, and we blow it all the time by just having fun. And I believe they are ready and willing to go deeper–we just don't do it. Frustrating!"
>
> –Volunteer from suburban Massachusetts

"THOSE ABOVE"

OTHER VOLUNTEERS

PARENTS

TEENAGERS

YOUTH WORK

YOU!

Example: Bible lesson on forgiveness

Hook: "See that poster paper on the wall? Grab a marker and write words that come to mind when you hear the word 'revenge.' "

Book: Use this section to read the text (Matthew 5:38-42); give a little background to the situation/place/people. Present a couple of points that would explain how the people who heard or read this first would understand it. (As mentioned already, I often have a student do this section, having worked with them in the week prior to get ready.)

Look: "Let's get in our small groups. We're thinking about revenge and forgiveness today, and we've looked at a couple of biblical examples of revenge gone bad. Think about people at school and your friends. What kind of issues come up, wrongs that people do to others, for which people want to get revenge?"

Took: "You've learned to trust each other over these weeks in your small groups. Share about a time recently when someone wronged *you*. Tell your group how you are doing at forgiving that person. When everyone has finished sharing, pray around the circle. Each person will pray for the person on your right. Pray that they'll be able to forgive and let go of the desire to get even."

Example: Bible lesson on miracles and God's power
Hook: "I am sure you noticed that you're sitting at round tables tonight. In a moment we're going to play a version of *Jeopardy!* For each question, the table that gets the answer right gets a prize. For example, here's a bag of sour licorice! OK, here we go. Category: Shocking Things Said by Whom? First item: 'Class, I've decided to give you all an "A" for this class.' " (Answer: Who is my teacher?)

Book: Use this section to read the text (such as Luke 5:17-24 and Romans 8:10-11) and give a little background to the situation, place, and people. Present a couple of points that would explain how the people who heard or read this first would understand it. (As mentioned already, I often have a student do this section, having worked with them in the week prior to get ready.)

Look: "Let's get in our small groups. We're thinking about shocking things, and we've looked at a couple of Jesus' miracles that made people drop-jawed amazed. We also looked at Paul's idea that the same power that raised Jesus from the dead lives in you as a Christian. Come up with some examples of what a real miracle would look like for you, your family, or your friends—or how things might be different for you this week if you really lived with Christ's power flowing through you."

Took: "OK, pick one thing that is specific as you look ahead to the coming week, one situation where you need God to show up and where you need power to face the situation. Then pray for each other."

"THOSE ABOVE"

OTHER VOLUNTEERS

PARENTS

TEENAGERS

YOUTH WORK

YOU!

CHAPTER 17

COUNSELING YOUTH

"THOSE ABOVE"

OTHER VOLUNTEERS

PARENTS

TEENAGERS

YOUTH WORK

YOU!

> *One of the top five reasons people enjoy volunteering in youth ministry: "I like it when they share their problems with me."*
> —*Volunteer Youth Workers Survey*

I was sitting at the dining room table when my oldest daughter came home from middle school.

"Hi, how was your day, MaryAnn?"

"Terrible." And with that she began heading up the stairs. I called out to her, "I'm sure things will get better!" (Sound of door slamming.)

From the kitchen came the voice of my wife, directed at me: "Nice job, Mr. Expert."

I realized what an idiot I had just been, marched up the stairs, and knocked on my daughter's door. She said I could come in.

"MaryAnn, I am so sorry! Please forgive me for what I just did. Could we start again? Tell me what happened."

And with that she started to explain, in some detail, what had gone wrong. Our conversation was off and running.

Sigh.

Many of us, as adults, have a default mode when it comes to a teenager sharing a vulnerability or problem. We give quick advice that closes the door to communication. We struggle to know how to help—when to just listen and when to try and give input. Few youth volunteers are trained as therapists or in counseling teenagers. But we can still be used of God in the lives of students when it comes to their problems and issues.

There is a simple, four-step model that can be helpful when it comes to helping teenagers through their issues. To illustrate, with a little humor, here is the same scenario repeated four times, each with a different response.

> ***"While I don't enjoy that kids have problems, it is a sacred thing when they let you into their world enough to share their problems and trials."***
> *–Volunteer from suburban Illinois*

Background: I'm a little early for the youth group meeting, setting things up. Jared walks in...normally he seems happy and smiling. Today, he looks the opposite.

Scenario One: Advice-Giving Response

Me: *Jared, what's up? You look kinda down tonight.*

Jared: *My girlfriend broke up with me.*

Me: *Oh, that's too bad. Well, there are other fish in the sea, as they say. I'm sure someone better will come along soon; just be patient.*

Is Jared going to open up and pour out his heart? Of course not! It is like he put in his nickel and got a nickel's worth of advice. My response did not open the door to communication; it slammed it shut. This response is called advice giving. Note: I am not saying we should avoid giving advice to students. I'm only saying when it comes to advice: *Not first.*

Scenario Two: Spiritualizing Response

Me: *Jared, what's up? You look kinda down tonight.*

Jared: *My girlfriend broke up with me.*

Me: *Oh, that's too bad. Well, just pray about it, and I'm sure Jesus will comfort you and you'll be back to normal in no time.*

Is Jared going to open up and pour out his heart? I doubt it. We've jumped right to a quick, spiritualized answer. This response I call spiritual input and reassurance. Is spiritual input and reassurance something we should give students? Of course it is...but *not first.*

Scenario Three: Identity Response

Me: *Jared, what's up? You look kinda down tonight.*

Jared: *My girlfriend broke up with me.*

Me: *Wait, what did you say?*

Jared: *My girlfriend broke up with me.*

Me: (long pause) *That is such a shocker. I mean, what happened, what did she say?*

Jared: *Last night I picked her up, we were going to get pizza and then study bio, but the first thing she said was "I don't want to be with you anymore and..."* (more explanation).

Me: *You must have been in shock. Did you see it coming?*

Jared: *I had no idea.*

Me: *I bet you didn't sleep so well last night.*

Jared: *You got that right and when I saw her in bio today...*(more explanation)

As you can see, this conversation is off and running...and if other students start to arrive I'd pull Jared aside and we'd agree to talk again after the meeting or on the phone later that night or the next day. In this scenario, the door of communication was flung wide open by what is called the identity response. I affirm the reality of his feelings and gently ask him to tell me about different aspects of it, as well as his feelings.

Scenario Four: Self-Revealing Response

Me: *Jared, what's up? You look kinda down tonight.*

Jared: *My girlfriend broke up with me.*

Me: *Oh, that's too bad. I remember when I was 14, Shelley broke up with me. We were very much in love. It's so weird to think about it now. We were planning on getting married, but she dumped me for my best friend. I hardly ate for a week, I was just so sick with sorrow, and at youth group I couldn't even look at her without feeling like crying in sadness or screaming in anger..."*

This is called the self-revealing response, and here I've used it too soon. Of course no teenager wants to hear, "Well, when I was your age..." but somewhere in the conversation, if we can honestly and authentically identify with either the situation or the emotion, we may, with discretion, reveal this as part of the conversation. Honesty and authenticity are vital here…don't make stuff up ("Well, when I was a drug dealer…"), as the teenager will probably sense it immediately.

An ideal sequence

While it is unfortunate that many adults either give advice first or jump right to spiritualizing first, neither really provides the teenager with healing and caring communication that may go well beyond a single conversation. You've probably already put it together yourself, but the ideal sequence is:

1. Identification Response (scenario 3)
2. Self-Revealing Response, if appropriate (scenario 4)
3. Advice-Giving Response (scenario 1)

   Sometimes I'll even ask the student after the first two stages have happened, "So, would like some input on this or were you just looking for someone to share the situation with?" Faced with this choice, most teenagers will now be glad for input.

4. Reassurance and Spiritual Input Response (scenario 2)

   Whether or not the student is a Christian, she or he may be very open to the offer for prayer support. A Christian student will likely be very open to all the resources, comfort, and hope we have in Christ.

"THOSE ABOVE"

OTHER VOLUNTEERS

PARENTS

"TEENAGERS"

YOUTH WORK

YOU!

THE WILDLIFE

Parents

A good field guide, if it is about any kind of living creature—birds, mammals, or even cold-blooded reptiles—will help us understand how this creature behaves in the wild. Knowledge helps us catch this creature, if that's our goal. As volunteer youth workers, we want to "catch" parents—to have them as active supporters of this ministry to their own sons and daughters. To do this we first need to understand parents as a species, how they think, and what is important to them. If you are already a parent yourself, you can compare your own feelings and experiences with the descriptions found in this section.

DIFFERENT PRESSURES

"THOSE ABOVE"

OTHER VOLUNTEERS

PARENTS

TEENAGERS

YOUTH WORK

YOU!

Parenting can be hard, frustrating, and unrewarding. Parents in the inner city may have extreme anxiety over the safety of their children day to day. Wealthy and educated parents may have extreme anxiety over their children being admitted to Ivy League schools. Many parents feel they've completely lost control of their teenagers and the Internet, media downloads, and social networking technology. They fear their son or daughter will make a mistake that will impair them for life. This parental fear and anxiety can actually be the thing that put parents on our side, however. We'll miss this opportunity if we don't pay attention to the fears and anxieties of parents. To ignore parents is to invite misunderstanding and conflict.

Life cycles and seasons

Parents aged 35-55 are experiencing many personal pressures. As the economy has globalized, many parents feel their employment is not secure. While their parents may have enjoyed a lifetime job with good benefits, many adults today face not only job insecurity but also declining health care benefits and increasing insurance costs.

Another pressure parents is face is health, or lack of it. The health of their own parents—grandparents to the students in your youth group—may be failing, particularly with issues stemming from decades of unhealthy eating and continuous weight gain. As the inescapable evidence mounts, parents conclude that their bodies will not last forever; they are mortal.

Marital stresses of parenthood

Add to the economic pressures the personal pressures of just trying to stay married. Many men and woman marry their opposites when it comes to personality and it's all very alluring and attractive at first. After a few years, however, those very differences require significant emotional energy to bridge, especially when times are tough. Those differences may become more acute and more stressful when a teenage child's attitudes or behaviors stray into negative territory. Life may not be what they pictured when they said "I do" so many years before. It is very difficult for parents to come to agreement on how to handle a child who has a bad attitude, displays a reckless streak, or struggles with substance abuse.

Feeling guilty

As two-income marriages have become the norm in North America, many parents feel guilty because they don't have enough time for their children. Parents may feel trapped: They want to make time with their children a greater priority, but they also want to maintain an income that funds the lifestyle the family enjoys.

Parental angst may mean openness to you

The upside of all these parenting challenges is that most parents know they need help. If we as volunteers set aside one hour every three months to research materials for parents of teenagers, we would be able to offer a range of helpful resources. The primary source to find these resources will likely come from websites and reviews of parent resources in books.[21]

One of the best thing we can do, especially if we are parents of teenagers ourselves, is to simply listen to parents. Remember the four-part communication sequence described in Chapter 17? We listen first, asking only questions related to how they felt about what has happened; then we can, if authentic, self-identify with a similar situation we have faced in our own parenting. Next, we may offer some advice and lastly spiritual comfort and spiritual perspective.

"THOSE ABOVE"

OTHER VOLUNTEERS

PARENTS

TEENAGERS

YOUTH WORK

YOU!

CHAPTER 19

PARENTS AND SAFETY

"THOSE ABOVE"

OTHER VOLUNTEERS

PARENTS

TEENAGERS

YOUTH WORK

YOU!

I shudder to think of the foolish and dangerous things I did with my youth group when I was a rookie youth worker—all in the name of excitement and, quite frankly, the quest to be cool and liked by the students.

- I once jammed 11 junior highers into my new Camaro (eight in the back, three in the front, including one on the gear stick). I thought I was cool, but the cop who pulled me over was less impressed.

- Our river rafting trip was supposed to be a day of fun in the sun. I was pleased that Tom, a disabled student, decided to come along. Life jackets didn't even cross my mind. About halfway through our trip along this river—cold, fast-moving (in places), milky water that came out of the glaciers of Mount Rainier— Tom's raft flipped. He did his best to hang on to a tree limb as other students swam to shore. I saw the fear in his face, and I felt fear in my heart as I realized the water was too deep and too fast for me to get to him. The minutes ticked by. I was getting very cold standing waist deep, hanging on to another limb—as close as I could get without being swept away myself. Then James appeared—a 12th-grader, excited to give his new wetsuit a try. He asked me if he could just float along behind us at his own pace. I told him, "Yes, why not?" James floated up behind Tom, grabbed him, and got to shore. I forded the river downstream, got to Tom and James, and was smart enough to realize Tom was hypothermic (turning blue gave it away). At least I remembered what the books say to do in a hypothermia situation. Tom eventually stopped shivering, and his color turned normal. We packed up our rafts and headed home. I tried not to think about what would have happened had James not been there.

- Our youth room in the church basement was large, about 40 by 100 feet. I thought it was a great idea to put black paper over the exit lights, push all of the furniture aside, and divide the group of 60 kids in half. I told them to line up on opposite walls and get on their hands and knees. The team that traversed the 100-foot distance to the opposite wall first would win. Simple enough, right? I then turned out all the lights. It was so dark, it was impossible to see your own hand in front of your face. "Go!"

  It never once occurred to me that someone might be injured... until two boys were...head to head, middle of the room. I turned on the lights. Fortunately, there were no broken necks, no brain trauma, and no lawsuits from families.

Parents like it when their children come home from youth group or youth events alive and uninjured. If we consistently demonstrate a reckless disregard for common safety practices, at the very least we'll lose credibility and support. At worst we may have to live with the knowledge that our own thoughtlessness caused permanent injury or harm to a teenager in our care.

We don't have to be strict, hard-nosed, fun-squelchers in youth ministry. Teenagers can have a great and exciting time without being put at risk. I eventually learned from my close calls and realized

I'd better get smart about safety.[22] Among the things that became "musts" for me:

- Seat belts used by all, in vans or cars.

- No games involving airway blockages (like Chubby Bunny).

- If the outside game involves running or chasing, make sure the area is free of construction or other debris. If we're playing basketball or any other court game, make sure there is nothing to trip on within about 20 feet of the court.

- Inside games involving running or chasing: Put away all tables and chairs in the area.

- Inside games involving darkness: No running or chasing.

- No games involving tackling.

If parents see we're responsible and careful when it comes to the safety of their sons and daughters, it builds bridges and credibility.

"THOSE ABOVE"

OTHER VOLUNTEERS

PARENTS

TEENAGERS

YOUTH WORK

YOU!

"THOSE ABOVE"

OTHER VOLUNTEERS

PARENTS

TEENAGERS

YOUTH WORK

YOU!

CHAPTER 20

ESPECIALLY FOR VOLUNTEERS UNDER AGE 25

Gaining the respect of the parents of teenagers is not an impossible mission for younger volunteers. True, it might be two decades before you are "in the shoes" of your students' parents, but there are insights that will help you understand parents. Beyond that, you can take proactive steps to build bridges with parents and gain respect in the process.

Adult behavior even if you don't feel like an adult

In church-based youth ministry, we will likely be invited by parents to a home or apartment for a meal. We may have a background in which "hospitality" was rarely practiced. In this social situation, it is important to know what constitutes adult behavior in a "home for a meal" scenario. I teach my youth ministry students that adult behavior in a home meal scenario generally includes these aspects: (1) When invited, immediately ask what you can bring (rolls? salad? a desert?), and if the answer is "nothing," be sure and bring a gift when you arrive, like flowers or nuts or candy; (2) arrive within 10 minutes of the stated time, having turned off all your electronic devices; (3) around the table, be sure and remember to pass the food to the next person when it comes your direction; and (4) be sure to engage younger children, if any, in conversation along with the teenagers and adults.

If you do offer to bring something and engage the younger siblings of the teenager, parents will definitely be thinking, "Wow! This is an adult!" This good impression will be passed on to others in the coming days. "We had Mary over the other night, and my, what a wonderful and mature young woman she is. I'm so glad she's working with our teenagers."

Be true to your word

Have you ever had a boss, a relative, or a pastor who, unfortunately, became famous for not being true to their own word? Not doing what we say we will do makes people confused at first; then it spirals into anger. If we tell a parent we're going to be touch with their son or daughter, woe to us if we forget.

If we tell a parent we're going to get back to them on something, not doing so will diminish our credibility. What kind of things do parents want to know about?

"Who will be the drivers for the event this coming Saturday?"

"Is the cooking staff of the retreat center sensitive to students with special dietary need such as... (lactose intolerance, peanut allergies, diabetes)?"

"Which volunteer youth workers have had first aid training, and where do you keep your first aid kit?"

"What's your policy for where students sleep on a camping trip? Do you allow them to sleep on the beach (or lawn) in one big group, or are the genders separated?"

"You have AAA® or some other automobile breakdown plan, right?"

"When do students sleep during lock-ins?"

"On normal youth group night, will the group always be at the church or do you sometimes go out for ice cream or do something else off site? Will I be notified in advance if you are going to leave the church building?"

Another thing parents appreciate is when your meetings and events conclude at the scheduled time. In American culture, time is as valuable as money, so making parents wait (about anything) communicates that we are inconsiderate. If an event is off site and you are going to be more than 15 minutes late, call or text the revised estimated time of arrival right away. Better yet, have a key parent contact who has agreed in advance to contact other parents.

> *"Parents complain that their youth don't like the youth ministry program; we do a survey and talk about what needs to change. We make the changes, but parents do not encourage their youth to come and start complaining all over again."*
>
> *—Volunteer from suburban Pennsylvania*

Communication

Parents like communication. Even if they are too busy to pay attention to our announcements, schedules, and other important information about the youth group, doing everything we can to help them stay informed is important. Most youth groups have pages as part of the church's website, where parents can get youth group event information.

"THOSE ABOVE"

OTHER VOLUNTEERS

PARENTS

TEENAGERS

YOUTH WORK

YOU!

> ## "Parents need to embrace their role as their children's primary catechist more seriously."
> – Volunteer from suburban Maryland

Appearance says something

I was once invited to be a guest speaker for three successive Thursdays at a nearby youth group. Each week, it struck me that the youth room was a total mess. There were unwashed (and cement-hard) paint brushes sitting on open paint cans from their youth room repainting efforts two months prior. The refreshment tables were sticky with some mystery substance? Wires and cords of all sorts were strewn around the front of the room...a few more, it seemed, each week. The place was a complete and utter mess.

The message this room gave was "This group has no adults in leadership." Am I saying a youth room has to be hospital-clean and library-organized? Of course not. But most adults, particularly parents, place a value on order.

Genuine appreciation

Parents love to hear good things about their sons and daughters. If you are able, try to have interaction with parents as students arrive or are picked up; just a quick sentence or two goes a long way. For example, as Ruth exits the passenger side when arriving at your event, you come to the driver side and say to her mom, "I want you to know how much we all appreciate Ruth. She is so helpful at cleanup time and so cheerful. That's gotta mean you're doing something right at home. Thanks a lot!"

If you really want to surprise a parent (and run the risk of parent heart attack!), write a note to express appreciation for their child.

OTHER VOLUNTEERS

PARENTS

TEENAGERS

YOUTH WORK

YOU!

THE WILDLIFE

Other Volunteers

A few weeks ago I had the fun of sitting back in youth group while Stephanie, another volunteer, led the games and Bible time for the night. She did an awesome job! What made this especially cool is that I remember her as a middle school student. I've had the fun of watching her grow up and now, as a university student, take leadership in the very same student ministry. I've had the joy of watching her spiritual gifts and strengths grow and blossom.

Of those who took the Youth Ministry Volunteer Survey, only 3 percent were working completely by themselves. Of the remaining, half were volunteering under the leadership of a paid (full time or part time) youth pastor or youth director. The other half were the "chief volunteer."

CHAPTER 21

IF YOU'RE "THE CHIEF"

> *"The person supervising me doesn't communicate well with me about the plans, schedule, and events of the youth group."*
> *—Volunteer Youth Workers Survey*

Congratulations, you're in management! Maybe you were at a church meeting. Maybe the person next to you was whispering a funny story. When she finished, you raised your hand to ask a question about the church building fund, but you hadn't heard the pastor ask, "Is God telling anyone here to lead our youth ministry?" Now you understand why there were cheers and applause when you raised you hand!

Well, however you got the job, you're the leader. As you know, there is a lot to think about. As "chief" we realize it takes skills to work with teenagers. We need to be able build relationships, lead games, make announcements, or teach. We need the ability to encourage, equip, and unleash our students into a life of serving God.

But as "chief" we also realize it take *an additional set of skills* to manage other volunteers and work with church staff. When I get the chance to speak about this topic in seminars, I like to ask, "Have you ever worked for a terrible boss? Without giving their name—

"THOSE ABOVE"

OTHER VOLUNTEERS

PARENTS

TEENAGERS

YOUTH WORK

YOU!

please, no gossip here—what made them a terrible boss from your point of view?"

Hands always shoot up when I ask this question, and the answers are always similar.

"He was terrible at communication...no one knew what he wanted us to do."

"He was so full of himself. For him, it was always 'My way or the highway.' "

"She thought we were all idiots and that only she had brains."

"For her it was a power thing. She had 'control' over us because she set the schedule."

May no one say these things about you!

> "*As the volunteer head of youth ministry, I have no staff person that I report to on a regular basis. I feel alone in doing ministry. I don't feel like I get the respect I should. I have no one to regularly encourage me and spiritually support me.*"
>
> *–Volunteer from suburban Michigan*

Here are six basic management skills or tasks. Develop and use them, and the people "under" you may be tempted to hoist you to their shoulders and shout, "Hosanna!"

1. Jesus in you

A foundation for everything, especially our ministry, is our own walk with Christ. It may be strange to include this as a "management skill," but our relationship with Christ is a foundation for everything we do. If we are overflowing with him, if we are "dwelling deep," we are able to look beyond the pressures of the day, the frustrations at work or home, and focus on presence-centered ministry with teenagers and the other volunteers. Jesus demonstrated so often the notion of servant leadership.

2. Management of time and space

Every situation is different, but time and space issues, at least for those of us holding youth group meetings in a church building, often include:

- Who arrives first? Does this person have a key? Who sets up chairs, tables, audio/video equipment, and sports equipment?
- Who cleans up at the end, and what constitutes "good enough" when it comes to clean?
- Who watches the clock...starts the meeting, keeps things on track to end on time?
- Is there any kind of "curriculum" plan? That is, if there is a "youth talk" or "Bible study" is it just one person who does this week after week, or is this rotated through the volunteers? In the youth group I lead, the other volunteers get a schedule in three-month blocks identifying who is in charge of games and other parts of the meeting. This year

"THOSE ABOVE"

OTHER VOLUNTEERS

PARENTS

TEENAGERS

YOUTH WORK

YOU!

we've focused on Philippians, unpacking a couple verses each week, and building a Hook Book Look Took teaching (see Chapter 14) from those verses.

If we are the chief, we do not necessarily have to do every aspect of the ministry ourselves, but if we make sure they get done, volunteers feel more secure. For example, for set-up, I usually arrive first because I'm the only one with the key. When the next volunteer comes we decide who will continue with set-up and who will just hang out with students as they arrive.

When I was a paid youth pastor, I did the major set-up earlier in the day. Now, as a volunteer, often I'm coming to youth group after an intense day at the office, a quick meal at home, and then a drive to church at which point the tiredness of the day nearly overwhelms me. Confession: Sometimes I stop at 7-Eleven® for a Snickers® or Caramello®. That, along with prayer ("Have mercy on me God!"), normally jump-starts my adrenaline so I'm fine by the time that first student walks through the door.

3. **The care and feeding of other volunteers**
How often do youth ministry volunteers meet to talk about the ministry? The survey included the statement "Youth ministry volunteers meet regularly together..." The responses were:
- Not really—25 percent
- Weekly—15 percent
- Twice monthly—5 percent
- About monthly—35 percent
- Less than monthly—20 percent

If you are the chief volunteer and have say over if and how often meetings happen, a monthly meeting at the minimum has the potential to accomplish several good things. Here is a meeting template many find helpful.

- Food and fellowship.
- Catching up and prayer. (I like to ask for each person to share something that made them smile or laugh in the last couple of days in their personal lives, apart from youth group. This is followed by sharing of prayer items, gratitude, or needs for the volunteers themselves, not for dear Aunt Martha and not even for the youth ministry. We then pray, in thanks or intercession.)
- Discuss how things have gone in our youth ministry since we last met.
- Calendar and planning items.
- Training. I copy an article from GROUP Magazine or a few pages from a training resource for us to read and discuss.
- Prayer. This prayer time is exclusively for the students and the youth ministry. If we are doing this in a carpeted room, I like to have us kneel during this prayer time.

I've notice that people like these meetings and feel cared for. We try to keep these meetings relaxed and fun, accomplish critical youth ministry tasks, and help people feel connected as partners in the ministry.

4. **Celebrating gifts and strengths**
Every volunteer in our ministry is gifted, has strengths, and should feel that their role in the ministry harnesses the strengths of their personality and God-given abilities. (See Chapters 3-5.) One way to help harness this is by delegating well.

"THOSE ABOVE"

OTHER VOLUNTEERS

PARENTS

TEENAGERS

YOUTH WORK

YOU!

Are you raising funds for the mission trip to Paris? (Paris, France, not Paris, Idaho.) Does the thought of keeping track of the donations and doing fundraisers make you lie awake at night in dread? There might be someone with "ant" organization qualities among your volunteers, or if not there, among the parents.

> *"I very much admire the youth pastor in our church for his love for God and passion for reaching youth. However, there is no sense of a 'team' feel. I don't know what other youth workers are doing or feeling, I don't know what upcoming events are and how I can help, and often I could have helped if I had known."*
>
> –Volunteer from suburban Alabama

Does the thought of leading youth group games give you a sick feeling in your stomach? Look for that outgoing "otter." She'll feel God singing over her when she's helping students have a good time through well-led games.

I'm not much of the counselor type. Yes, I care about the teenagers and don't mind if they tell me their problems and stresses. But I love to recruit other volunteers who *live* to listen to hearts of youth and help bring healing to hurting.

Occasionally I meet youth workers who have the astounding notion that they alone possess all the gifts and abilities that are needed in youth ministry. If they have "helpers," those individuals simply come to youth group and stand around watching The Man (or The Woman) do what he/she thinks they're good at. I'm aware of this because I used to be that person, but over the years I received increasingly negative feedback from people. Eventually, and painfully, I was able to renounce the "I can do it all" syndrome.

If we're the chief volunteer, one of our roles is to discern what others are good at. Once strengths and gifts are known, delegate and celebrate, affirm and unleash. It is amazing how motivated people become in ministry when they feel cared for and feel they are getting the opportunity to do what they were born to do.

5. **Clear purpose and clear expectations**
   If your youth ministry has no statement of mission or vision, get a good cup of coffee or a can of Red Bull® from the fridge, do some serious praying, and put some thoughts down. Here is one example that works for the youth group I lead.

Living Christ Church Middle School Ministry
Mission/Vision/Core Values

The mission of LCC's Middle School Ministry is to support the kingdom-centered mission of Living Christ Church, in helping middle school students love mercy, act justly, and walk humbly with their God.

The vision of LCC's Middle School Ministry is to accomplish the mission through the pattern of ministry Jesus modeled in the Gospels: Win/Build/Equip/Unleash.

"THOSE ABOVE"

OTHER VOLUNTEERS

PARENTS

TEENAGERS

YOUTH WORK

YOU!

Core Values

- **Intentional:** Everything we do will fit into one or more of these areas: win, build, equip, unleash.
- **Student-Centered:** God uses teenagers; we intend to harness the gifts and talents of middle school students. They will not be simply spectators.
- **Team:** No one leader has all the gifts/strengths for ministry. Every adult volunteer will be able to use their gifts/talents with joy.
- **Spirit-Led:** We affirm it is only by prayer, Christ's power, and the Spirit's leading that God will "show up" in the ministry. We long to see things that can only be explained by God himself.
- **Whole-Church Focus:** We seek to integrate teenagers into the life and ministry of the whole church.
- **Parents in the Loop:** Communication a high priority

If this were your youth ministry, the next step would simply be a section where you write down how the pieces of your ministry (I call them program components) fit into your stated purposes. You'll notice the example I've given states that our vision involves a process: build/equip/win/unleash. This is how I laid it out when I was designated the main volunteer:

How Program Components Fit into the Vision

Build: *For the purpose of spiritual growth, and fellowship/ encouragement.*

Program components:
- Sunday school
- Wednesday youth group
- Occasional group outreach events

Equip: *For the purpose of having students minister, not just be ministered to.*

Program components:
- Student Leadership Team...to plan group events and have other input. Meets monthly.
- Service Project Ministry: Once every five weeks on Wednesday.
  - Adopt a Grandparent
  - Cooking (giving fresh cookies to prayer meeting attenders as a thank you)
- Sunday Worship Service involvement: Scripture reading, testimony, music team
- Outreach Night: once every five weeks...a Wednesday evening completely led by the students themselves. No adults up front, period.

Win: *For the purpose of giving church students a venue in which they can invite friends and see them come to Christ.*

Program components:
- Outreach night once every five weeks
- Multi-church outreach events
- The regular youth group meeting will be sensitive to the unchurched

Unleash: *For the purpose of letting teenagers use their own gifts and talents.*

Program components:
- Student Leadership Team
- Outreach Ministries (once every five weeks)
- Service Project Ministries (once every five weeks)

"THOSE ABOVE"

OTHER VOLUNTEERS

PARENTS

TEENAGERS

YOUTH WORK

YOU!

Here one more idea for you as chief. Though it may seem obvious or unnecessary, it is amazing how positive the impact of a well-written ministry job description can be. When used as a recruiting tool, it gives people confidence the ministry is well led. For ongoing staff, it provides clear direction of expectation, even if someone is only giving a few hours a week to the ministry.

6. Defining volunteer roles

Please note: Ideas for the description below did not come only out of my own head. Over the years I've borrowed and adapted pieces of this structured description as a kind of template. I find that volunteers like to see how what they do connects to a larger purpose, along with specifics as to what is actually expected. And everyone likes to know they can be successful!

The "purpose" connects the youth ministry to the mission of the church. "Responsibilities" include not only expectations for the ministry, but also for the growth of the volunteer. "Length of commitment" helps people realize this is not a "till death do us part situation. "You'll know you're succeeding when..." helps people feel like they can be successful.

Living Christ Church
Middle School Ministry Position Description
Weekly Youth Group Meeting Staff*

Purpose
To serve the Lord in helping fulfill the mission of Living Christ Church through winning, building, equipping, and unleashing middle school students for Jesus Christ.

Responsibilties

- For your own growth
    1. Be a regular and active participant of Living Christ church.
    2. Attend the monthly Adult Staff meeting.
    3. Read provided resources to encourage you spiritually and upgrade your ministry skills (such as smallyouthgroup.com).

- For your ministry
    1. Attend weekly youth group meeting to build relationships with students and lead or assist as your giftedness and passions make clear.
    2. Pray for a subset of the group on a regular basis.
    3. Rotate to non-Wednesday events (outreach/fellowship) according to an agreed-upon schedule.

- Length of commitment
    1. Through the youth group calendar year... September-July.

You'll know you are succeeding when...

1. You know the students' names and something about them.
2. They actually talk with you.
3. You enjoy them, and they seem to enjoy you.
4. You grow in finding out what aspect of this ministry you feel most gifted in and most passionate about.
5. You have a sense of team ministry with the other adult staff.
6. You look forward to Wednesday night.
7. The youth and the ministry start coming to mind during the week "out of the blue."

"THOSE ABOVE"

OTHER VOLUNTEERS

PARENTS

TEENAGERS

YOUTH WORK

YOU!

*All volunteer staff must fill out the normal church volunteer application, which includes granting permission for a criminal background check.

Curious about the "volunteer application?" Nearly 60 percent of the survey respondents had to go through some sort of application process to make their volunteering in the church officially approved. Most denominations and independent churches have volunteer application guidelines and procedures. The primary purpose is to protect children and youth from pedophiles, child abusers, and sexual predators.[23]

A SURPRISING ROLE FOR ALL VOLUNTEERS

"THOSE ABOVE"

OTHER VOLUNTEERS

PARENTS

TEENAGERS

YOUTH WORK

YOU!

Armed with the insights and ideas of this field guide, you'll be a better volunteer. Perhaps, for example, you can help others know about the Cerebral Upgrade (Chapter 10) or you can see that Hook Book Look Took (Chapter 14) will help you and other volunteers more effectively teach the Bible for life change.

> *"Talk with those above you and get clear information about what is expected of you. Love the teens you work with no matter how they look or how much they frustrate you."*
>
> *–Volunteer from rural New York*

Here is an important subject we haven't talked about yet but is potentially helpful no matter where we may fit in our church or youth ministry:

Biblical reconciliation and peacemaking

Ever seen a dispute or conflict nearly ruin a relationship, a youth ministry, or a whole church? Sadly, many of us have. I researched for a previous book what kind of things caused youth pastors to lose their jobs. Conflict was reason No. 1.[24] Ken Sandy of Peacemaker

Ministries points out that each of us a "style" when it comes to conflict.[25] Peacemaker Ministries produces training materials and resources to help churches whose members are in severe conflict, as well as individuals who are in conflict with others in the home, the extended family, or the workplace.

Denying and running: Some of us (including me) tend to deny, ignore, or run from conflict. The usual result of avoidance is that understanding and reconciliation seldom happen. People are wounded. While some people (lions and otters, for example) tend to forget wrongs done to them, others (golden retrievers and ants) seldom forget the wrongs done to them. For these kind of people, a relationship cannot be normalized unless the "issue" is dealt with.

Anger and attacking: Some of us rather enjoy conflict and speaking up when we feel something is not right. If the situation warrants, we slide into anger, go into "attack" mode, and let people have it. Unfortunately this often produces defensiveness or an even angrier attack in response.

Neither approach to conflict leads to understanding and a restoration of relationship. Most of us have experienced broken relationships in our families or among friends. We may have seen a youth group devolve into fighting factions over an offhanded comment or a wounding put-down. Here are a few of the basic ideas that Peacemaker Ministries teaches in its seminars and through its DVD series for small groups called "The Peacemaking Church."

- **Conflict is an opportunity.**
  Yes, it is hard, but we have great resources in Scripture as well as a powerful and loving God who can work through us and others to transform an awful situation. For example,

in 1 Corinthians 10:31 Paul says this: *So whether you eat or drink, or whatever you do, do it all for the glory of God.* Certainly "whatever you do" would include dealing with conflict situations.

- **Living at peace is a key to being a Christian.**
  We can't escape the notion in Scripture that followers of Christ are to be at peace and in unity with one another and that we are to put reconciliation ahead of worship. (If you find that idea shocking, reread Matthew 5:23-24. Our unity, as Christians, is a key hallmark of our witness.)

- **When we are in conflict, our own "idols" are revealed.**
  This really hits home for me. Our desires turn into demands, which lead to judging, which leads to punishing. (Example of punishing: the silent treatment.)

- **Confession brings freedom.**
  Realizing and admitting our own faults is the first step in reconciliation. "I realize I was wrong when I [be specific], and I ask for your forgiveness."

- **Gently restoring someone and a relationship is *mission possible*.**
  If we take responsibility for our own contribution to a conflict situation, the other person may readily admit their role or at least be able to "hear" how you experienced what took place.

- **In serious matters, have one or two other trusted (and wise) persons present for a conflict resolution and reconciliation gathering.** Both Jesus and the Apostle Paul talk about this (Matthew 18:15-17; 1 Corinthians 6:4).

"THOSE ABOVE"

OTHER VOLUNTEERS

PARENTS

TEENAGERS

YOUTH WORK

YOU!

We have ample opportunity to see conflict and experience it ourselves in life. We (yes, you and I) can be used as peacemakers.

THE WILDLIFE

"Those Above"

There is one last species to consider in *The Volunteer's Field Guide to Youth Ministry*. To whom do we report? About half of the surveyed respondents had a full-time or part-time paid youth worker above them. For the other half, the "just above" person is a pastor, priest, church leader, or leadership board.

UNDERSTANDING THOSE ABOVE

"THOSE ABOVE"

OTHER VOLUNTEERS

PARENTS

TEENAGERS

YOUTH WORK

YOU!

Nickels and noses

The person above us may not have the same list of priorities as we do. They may have a bigger picture in view.

Senior pastors and priests may be preoccupied with a budget shortfall (nickels). Maybe attendance is down again this year (noses). They may feel discouraged that a key family has moved away. Perhaps they are shaken by the news that a mega-church 20 miles away has announced plans for a daughter church and the new location is three blocks from your church building. Or perhaps the person just above your pastor or priest is a terrible leader and is causing great stress.

We don't necessarily see this bigger picture and the potential stressors to our supervisor. I try to pray for the person above me daily.

> *"The biggest frustration I have is communication from the pastor. I am directly below him, but rarely do I know what major church business is going on."*
>
> *–Volunteer from suburban Oregon*

Personality set points

A powerful key to getting along with whoever is above us is to understand what comes naturally to them: their strengths, personality, and gifts. Research from the world of management studies tell us that the No. 1 reason people resign and leave their jobs is that they cannot get along with the person just above them. Ministry settings are no exception to this.

The survey for this field guide summarized the four personality styles and asked people to indicate the main personality style of the person just above them. Here are the results:

Main Personality Style of the Person "Just Above" You

- Leader (lions)—48 percent
- Fun-Loving (otters)—19 percent
- Personally Caring (golden retrievers)—19 percent
- Detailed, Analytical (ants)—14 percent

If we have the same personality style as the person above us, we most often will think they are wonderful! After all, they think and act like we do—who wouldn't like that? If they are the opposite of us, watch out—there might be some stress in store for us.

When I was a youth pastor, one of the pastors I served under was the classic golden retriever (personally caring). The congregation loved him, and wow, was he a good counselor. Furthermore, he was amazing at funerals (no kidding). He had people telling him, a decade or two in advance, "When I die I want you to do my funeral." No one has ever said that to me (and I'm rather glad), but for him, it wasn't uncommon.

What drove me crazy, however, was that he had a very difficult time making decisions. The more important the decision, the harder it was for Andy make a decision. He wanted every decision to please everyone all the time. This was a large church and there were times when the other pastors on the staff (five of us) simply outvoted him. No, we didn't take votes, but when it came time to making big decisions, if five of us said yes but Andy felt it should be no, he sometimes relented. He would joke, "Well, you guys take the flack if this flops." I really respected him for that flexibility.

Over the years, I've learned to appreciate the strengths of the persons just above me. Sometimes I have to say to myself, "That's not how I would have done that…but that is OK!"

If we ourselves are a leader/lion, the pickiness of a "just above" ant/detailed-analytic may be discouraging because this person can never, it seems, get enough information to approve our visions and plans.

If we are a fun/otter person and the leader above us is a caring/ golden retriever person, we may ache to see more creativity and innovation in this person who values stability and security so dearly.

If we are a caring/golden retriever and our "just above" is a leader/ lion, we'll probably be put off by their assertiveness and the impression that they seem to have zero need for input. They make decisions without, it seems, any consideration for the feelings and needs of others.

If we are a detailed/analytic/ant, the fun (otter) "just above" may drive us mad with their disorganization, spontaneity, and fun simply for the sake of fun.

"THOSE ABOVE"

OTHER VOLUNTEERS

PARENTS

TEENAGERS

YOUTH WORK

YOU!

No surprises, please

Those above us don't like surprises. They don't want to hear bad news from someone else.

Early in the school year we had to prohibit two students from coming to youth group because their behavior was so out of bounds and dangerous to others. As "chief" volunteer I phoned the pastor to let him know what happened and why we made the decision we did. He was sad for the stress of it all but glad for the communication. These two boys were from the community but not from church families. (Three months later they returned repentant and re-entered the group.)

Late one night at a weekend retreat, I managed to back the church van into a tree, putting an almost perfect "V" into the bumper. No injuries...well, maybe 100 years from now people will gaze up at that tree and wonder what in the world happened to the poor thing. We drove back to the church just fine the next day. I called the office manager of the church; she was the main communication point with our insurance person. She mentioned it to the pastor and the trustee chairperson, as I expected she would. It wasn't a big deal, but the last thing I wanted was one of these "above" people to walk by the van and wonder what idiot damaged the van and didn't fess up.

I planned to take our youth group up into Canada for a snow and ski weekend. I signed the contract for the retreat center six months in advance of the event, and agreed upon a per person price in Canadian dollars. In the six months that followed the American dollar dropped about 15 percent compared to the value of the Canadian currency. This currency value change cost us an extra $500 (U.S.) on the trip compared to what was expected. If it were

$50 extra, no problem. A $500 extra expense was a problem. I phoned the church treasurer and explained it all. I put it in writing to him also, with a copy to the board chair and the pastor. I knew from previous experience that especially the money people in the church like to know exactly what happened when something does not go according to plan with finances.

If we are volunteering under a youth pastor, she or he will definitely want to know if there is an intense personal conflict within our small group that could erupt into the larger fellowship. She'll want to know if Cheryl seems uncharacteristically "down" or if there seems to be big problems in Jeremy's family. In large churches the youth pastor may not already know about these situations because there are just too many students to know them all personally.

"THOSE ABOVE"

OTHER VOLUNTEERS

PARENTS

TEENAGERS

YOUTH WORK

YOU!

BUILDING BRIDGES TO THOSE ABOVE

·THOSE ABOVE·

OTHER VOLUNTEERS

PARENTS

TEENAGERS

YOUTH WORK

YOU!

Visible youth

Each time our middle school ministry has a "Service Project Ministries" night, half the group visits an older adult or senior citizen. As it turns out, some of these people are in leadership positions of the church. On the way to the house, I ask the students to think of questions they would like to ask. The girls often want to hear about "How did you meet?" or "How did he propose?" or "What did you do on your first date?" The boys like to hear about danger— especially if the husband has ever been in the military. Several weeks ago we visited a prominent attorney who was also a judge. The boys were *very interested* about sending people to jail.

While half the group is visiting a member of the congregation, the other half is baking cookies in the church kitchen. Early in the evening one of the leaders heads upstairs to count how many are at prayer meeting that night. We creep silently into the back of the room (no easy task with 11- to 13-year-olds) with exactly the number of plates of cookies as there are people at prayer meeting. When we hear the last "amen," the students enter en masse and hand these plates of cookies to people as a thanks for their prayer ministry in the church. Wow! In a small church like ours, this simple act of kindness builds bridges like crazy.

> *"We are a small church with many older members. We try to get the kids involved more, but at times the 'traditional' view of the members makes it hard to try new things. We also have a very small budget, and a lot of what we do, the leaders pay for out of their own pockets"*
>
> *–Volunteer from rural Nebraska*

It is so easy for adults, especially older ones, to think that teenagers are lost, selfish, or don't care about anything or anyone else in the church. "Service project ministries" have helped us find an effective counterbalance to that view. Additionally, we have junior high and high school youth involved in the Sunday morning service—on the greeting team, collecting the offering, as Scripture readers, and on the worship team. When someone says "youth ministry" at a board meeting or at other adult functions, people picture these students and what they are doing in and for the church.

In one church I served as youth pastor, there was a building project that was being done mostly by the people of the church, under the supervision of a contractor. Every few weeks I held a special Saturday morning youth event (breakfast and basketball, breakfast and Nerf® ball wars...that sort of thing). We always ended this event with 30-60 minutes at the construction site doing cleanup. When 40 students attack a huge pile of construction rubbish, it really doesn't take very long to move it to the humongous metal trash containers in the church parking lot.

I heard a denominational youth director lament, "In the U.S. armed forces, we let 19-year-olds drive tanks worth $30 million; in our churches we don't let anyone under 25 do anything." We can be the ones to help advocate for youth within the church and help teenagers see serving the body as a necessary and positive thing.

Communication
You don't have to create a 20-page formal report in a three-ring binder every month, but you should, either verbally or in writing, give the "just above" person a summary of what happens on a regular basis. I know some youth workers provide copies of anything they send to the parents to the board members and pastor. These people may be, unfortunately, too busy to read what we send them, but we can't be accused of not trying to keep them in the loop. Here a small amount of time on our part can pay dividends in goodwill.

Only good in public
We may think our pastor or priest is a horrible preacher. But that opinion is not appropriate to share with others, not even as a prayer request. "Let's really pray for our pastor; he is so boring!" Over the years, people have said something like that to me about our preacher. Even if I agree, I never say so. Instead, I say something like, "I appreciate all the time and effort he obviously takes in preparation. I pray for him regularly. You, too?"

Nothing will poison a relationship like when someone above us hears that we are complaining about them to others. If that is the case we need to confess our gossip.

Honest affirmation
It is very helpful if we look for the good and positive things in the person just above us. When I work up enough courage to speak

"THOSE ABOVE"

OTHER VOLUNTEERS

PARENTS

TEENAGERS

YOUTH WORK

YOU!

personally to a supervisor about something negative about them, I begin talking about the strengths and virtues I see. I then say something like: "Something is on my mind, and I want to help you, who are very good, be even better! Would that be OK?" It's funny, because I've never had someone say, "No! I don't want to hear it!"

If a supervisor's experience of me has been one of support and affirmation over the long haul, they'll already know I'm not coming with a sledge hammer or stick of dynamite; they know from experience that I mean well.

A POSTSCRIPT FOR THE LONG-HAUL VOLUNTEER

Frankly I was quite amazed when I saw the stats from our survey indicating nearly 50 percent of the respondents had been volunteering in youth ministry 10 years or longer.

Throughout this book, the sidebars and quotes have revealed the heart and passion of those who love teenagers, despite the challenging aspects of youth ministry volunteering. I hope you have found and will continue to find this field guide a source of knowledge for your ministry and life. Knowledge helps us know both what to do and what not to do. It helps us be realistic about what to expect and how to save ourselves from grief and disappointment as we build fences against failure. Knowledge helps us soar as well.

Recently, I was talking about the Cerebral Upgrade (Chapter 10) with a group of youth workers. Tyrone raised his hand, stopping me in mid-sentence. "I feel like you've just taken this incredibly heavy burden off my shoulders." That's what knowledge can do…blessed by God it can help us soar.

> "*I love being with kids. They are so alive! On Tuesday I work with our senior high and on Wednesday our junior high. I have a long history with them because I know them from 7th - 12th and then we become friends when they are 20 and go to lunch together! And then I go to their weddings! I enjoy walking alongside them for that part of their lives when they are with us. I love to plan events, organize, execute. I love to lead Bible studies. I love Prison Dodgeball.*"
> —Volunteer from suburban Massachusetts

But we know there is more to youth ministry than knowledge. The mystical, spiritual, Holy Spirit part of ministry. We cannot put God in a box. We do not believe in a God who is predictable, who is always "safe." When God shows up, things happen that cannot be explained by training, knowledge, planning, personality, or anyone's smartness.

There's a verse in Isaiah that is particularly amazing to me. The passage is a very big deal, because Jesus quotes from it when explaining his own sense of call to the cynical, skeptical, or just plain confused people around him at the beginning of his ministry.

Jesus quotes this passage in Luke 4:18-19. The words come from Isaiah 61:1.

The Spirit of the Sovereign Lord is upon me, for the Lord has anointed me to bring good news to the poor. He has sent me to comfort the brokenhearted and to proclaim that captives will be released and prisoners will be freed.

But there's more! What comes next in Isaiah 61:2-3 strikes me as a description of God-breathed youth ministry:

He has sent me to tell those who mourn that the time of the Lord's favor has come, and with it, the day of God's anger against their enemies. To all who mourn in Israel, he will give a crown of beauty for ashes, a joyous blessing instead of mourning, festive praise instead of despair. In their righteousness, they will be like great oaks that the Lord has planted for his own glory.

Whenever I get discouraged as a youth worker, I remember that God, through the Holy Spirit, is working even when I can't see him. I'm being used of him to undo the ashes, mourning, and despair our culture generates in many teenagers. God is using *you* as well. We are, together as youth workers, being used of God to *give a crown of beauty for ashes, a joyous blessing instead of mourning, festive praise instead of despair.*

The result? They will be called oaks of righteousness, a planting of the Lord for the display of his splendor.

Thinking about this makes me want to smile with gratitude. You, too? Enjoy the journey as you've chosen to be a youth ministry volunteer!

ENDNOTES

1. A good resource on this topic is Archibald Hart's book *The Hidden Link Between Adrenaline and Stress* (Nashville, TN: Thomas Nelson, 1995).

2. See *NurtureShock: New Thinking About Children* by Po Bronson and Ashley Merryman (New York: Twelve Books, 2009). See especially Chapter 9.

3. A good introduction to this research can be seen in *NurtureShock;* see especially Chapter 8 "Can Self-Control Be Taught?" and Chapter 9 "Plays Well With Others." Also in this genre of current parenting research and literature you'll find *The Trophy Kids Grow Up* by Ron Alsop (New York: Jossey-Bass, 2008); *The Blessing of B Minus* by Wendy Mogel (New York: Scribner, 2010); and *Free Range Kids: How to Raise Safe, Self-Reliant Children (Without Going Nuts With Worry)* by Lenore Skenazy (New York: Jossey-Bass, 2010).

4. This chapter was adapted from my book *The Youth Ministry Survival Guide* (Grand Rapids, MI: Zondervan, 2008).

5. The animal framework was first published by Gary Smalley and John Trent in their marriage book *The Two Sides of Love* (Carol Stream, IL: Tyndale, 2006). I have changed their original term Beaver to Ant because the former word can sometimes be used in ways that are not appropriate for polite society. You also can find information by simply typing the words "Lion, Otter, Golden Retriever" into an online search engine.

6. Jerome Kagan, *Galan's Prophecy: Tempermant in Human Nature* (Boulder, CO: Westview Press, 1995).

7. Yes, some see these listed as suggestive only, while others see them as definitive. Online spiritual gift tests, explanations, and assessments abound. One example can be found at churchgrowth.org.

8. The simplest way to get the list and the strength definitions is to use a search engine for the phrase "strengthsfinder definitions." The actual link to the Gallup Management Journal page about this is:

   http://gmj.gallup.com/content/102310/clifton-strengthfinder-book-center.aspx

9. The easiest way to get more information is to consult respected online resources, including webmd.com or mayoclinic.com.

10. For an excellent discussion of the signs and symptoms of teenage depression see http://helpguide.org/mental/depression_teen.htm.

11. Christian Smith and Melissa Denton, *Soul Searching: The Religious and Spiritual Lives of American Teenagers* (New York: Oxford University Press USA, 2005).

12. Rick Warren, *Purpose Driven Church*, (Grand Rapids, MI: Zondervan, 1995).

13. Doug Fields, *Purpose Driven Youth Ministry*, (Grand Rapids, MI: Zondervan, 1998).

14. Len Kageler, "A Cross National Analysis of Church Based Youth Ministry." Presented as a plenary paper of the International Association for the Study of Youth Ministry, Cambridge, 2007, and published in the *Journal of Youth and Theology,* April 2010.

15. John Medina, *Brain Rules: 12 Principles for Surviving and Thriving at Home, Work, and School* (Seattle: Pear Press, 2008). See also Brainrules.net. Medina's 12 Brain Rules are: 1) Exercise boosts brain power, 2) The human brain evolved, too, 3) Every brain is wired differently, 4) We don't pay attention to boring things, 5) Repeat to remember, 6) Remember to repeat, 7) Sleep well, think well, 8) Stressed brains don't learn the same way, 9) Stimulate more of the senses, 10) Vision trumps all other senses, 11) Male and female brains are different, and 12) We are powerful and natural explorers.

16. One of my favorites is by Gary Smalley and John Trent, *The Two Sides of Love* (Tyndale, 2005).

17. I recommend *Speaking to Teenagers*, by Doug Fields and Duffy Robbins (Grand Rapids, MI: Zondervan, 2007) for great insight on giving youth talks.

18. Web resources include egadideas.com, ymtoday.com, simplyyouthministry.com, group.com, youthspecialties.com, and studentlife.com.

19. Howard Hendricks, *Teaching to Change Lives: Seven Proven Ways to Make Your Teaching Come Alive* (Portland, OR: Multnomah Press, 1987).

20. The percentages come out differently in different studies, but the variation is only minor. One study showed 30 percent were analytic learners, 28 percent dynamic, 25 percent relational, and 17 percent common sense. See http://madeinatlantis.com/life/learning_style.htm. The major takeaway is that the strong majority of teenagers do not learn best with the "sit and listen" approach to teaching.

21. A great comprehensive resource is the Center of Parent/Youth Understanding, CPYU.org. To know what's going on with movies, my favorite source is kidsinmind.org. They actually rate every movie in terms of sexual content, language, and violence. Also provided are the actual counts or cases of the occurrences of items in these three categories. For example, I know the movie *Hurt Locker* has lots of profanity in it, including 73 uses of the F-word. By contrast, *High School Musical 3: Senior Year* includes not a single swear word. The two instances of "sexual content" are when a boy and girl kiss.

22. For more thoughts, see Jack Crabtree's book, *Better Safe Than Sued* (Grand Rapids, MI: Zondervan, 2008).

23. A good resource for volunteers, including volunteer applications, is churchvolunteercentral.com.

24. Len Kageler, *The Youth Ministry Survival Guide.*

25. Peacemaker Ministries: Peacemaker.net. Adaptation used by permission.

APPENDIX 1

Volunteer Youth Workers Survey, Fall 2009

Gender
- Female—57%
- Male—43%

Marital Status
- Single—24%
- Married—76%

Age
- Under 20—3%
- 21-24—5%
- 25-29—9%
- 30-35—12%
- 36-40—14%
- 41-45—14%
- 46-50—19%
- 51-60—20%
- 61 and over—4%

Years in Youth Ministry
- Under 1 year—3%
- 1-3 years—15%
- 4-6 years—20%
- 7-10 years—17%
- More than 10 years—45%

Denomination
- Roman Catholic—16%
- Protestant—76%
- Para-Church—8%

Are you the "chief" volunteer?
- Yes—51%
- No—49%

Who is "just above" you?
- Another volunteer—8%
- A paid youth pastor/director—47%
- An elder or some other church leader—5%
- A pastor or priest—36%

The youth ministry you volunteer in is:
- Combined junior and senior high—56%
- Junior high only—16%
- Senior high only—15%
- Other—13%

How many hours per week do you devote to youth ministry?
- 1-2 hours—18%
- 2-4 hours—31%
- 4-6 hours—20%
- More than 7 hours—31%

If all youth who would typically come to something at least occasionally were in one place at one time, how many would that be?
- Under 10—11%
- 10-20—22%

- 20-30—30%
- 40-75—20%
- 75+—18%

When you became a volunteer, was there some kind of screening process?

- Yes—56%
- No—44%

Youth ministry volunteers in your setting meet regularly together...

- Not really—25%
- Weekly—15%
- Twice monthly—5%
- About monthly—35%
- Less than monthly—21%

What are some of your frustrations as a youth ministry volunteer? (You may choose up to three items.)

- 43%—I'm so busy with the rest of my life, sometimes it's overwhelming to try to be with kids, too.
- 21%—There are unclear expectations of what I'm supposed to be doing.
- 20%—I feel undervalued in my church as a youth worker.
- 18%—Unruly kids ruin for me.
- 16%—The person above me does not communicate well with me about plans/schedule/expectations.
- 12%—I don't have a good feel for my own strengths and gifts.
- 10%—I don't know their language/music/technology.
- 10%—I haven't been trained well to do what I'm supposed to do.
- 24% of responders selected "other." If they narrated this "other" the response usually was a combination of the ones listed.

What are some of the things you enjoy most about youth ministry? (You may choose up to three items.)

- 76%—Seeing kids "get it."
- 60%—Feeling that I'm contributing to our church and the kingdom by "being there" for these youth.
- 45%—Hanging out with kids.
- 40%—Being able to teach or lead.
- 34%—When kids share their problems with me.
- 30%—Worshipping alongside them.
- 30%—The special events/retreats.
- 24%—Working behind the scenes to make things go smoothly.

Personality sometimes depends on the situation, but what do you consider you home base...that is, where you are most comfortable most of the time. Select only one.

- Leader—34%
- Personally Caring—27%
- Detailed/Analytical—21%
- Fun/Outgoing—18%

APPENDIX 2

What Youth Workers Want

The survey included an open question that invited reflection: "If you could change *two things* about the youth ministry you are involved in, what would those two things be?"

Three-hundred respondents took the time to share their thoughts. Below you'll find a sampling of the things they would change if they could. You'll see they are grouped by section of the field guide. Chances are, you will find comments you would echo. If so, know that you are not alone in this journey of ministry to teenagers.

Part 1—You!

"I would let go of some of my insecurities so that I could better encourage and get to know the youth." —Suburban North Carolina

"It would have been nice to transition in when the director was not facing difficult circumstances. I would be able to work in my gift set." —Suburban Georgia

"My own dedication to the ministry. I need more inner drive to do a better job." —Rural Texas

"Focus more on personal walk/knowing God personally/how to do that." —North Carolina

Part 2—The "Field" of Youth Ministry

"Joint youth/adult leadership. Clear objectives." —Suburban New Mexico

"Better fit between me and the pastor in terms of values, vision, philosophy of youth ministry." —Urban Minnesota

"More opportunities for the 'church kids' rather than just for the seekers." —Rural Tennessee

"Expand Service/Justice Issues—Get them working and off the computer and/or games—Want self-esteem? Value? Purpose? Serve where you are gifted now—Don't WAIT!" —Urban Ohio

"That we focus on giving out to the community more. That the leaders share that desire and push the kids to do work for people other than themselves." —Urban California

"Have more of a plan/goal/mission statement." —Rural Pennsylvania

Part 3—Teenagers

"I would split junior high and high school so that each group would be more of an impact for their age group." —Suburban North Carolina

"More parents involved in their youth's spiritual development; divide the youth group down some—we have sixth grade through 12th grade youth." —Rural Maryland

"We need to find a way to make all kids feel a 'part' of the group. It breaks my heart to have kids quit coming, because the kids don't include them. I want to find a way to make them feel like we care if they are not there. They are missed. When you are dealing with teens, this is very hard." —Rural Texas

"I'd like to have a better handle on how to deal with the fringe kids; some are just loners, but others are intentionally disruptive." —Suburban Iowa

"I would get very serious about the issue of disrespecting the Lord, i.e. talking and messing around during times of worship. There is nothing wrong with cracking jokes and being lively, but there is a time and place for everything." —Suburban Georgia

"I think that kids need to be surveyed to see what peer pressure they are facing at earlier ages so that we can direct the Scripture to and the lessons to help them deal with the world today." —Suburban Florida

"More pure fellowship time with our small groups as opposed to 100 percent Bible study. We meet in gender-specific and age-specific small groups (I work with ninth-, 10th-grade boys) each Wednesday night, and it's a great way for those students to grow together. I wish we'd do more socially as a group, though, to give them time to really grow together outside of Bible study as well." —Suburban Illinois

"Maturity level of the kids. I have the most unruly bunch, and they are hard for me to handle on my own." —Suburban Oregon

Part 4—Parents

"To be more informed on upcoming youth events in our church."
—Suburban Texas

"Wish more kids were trained by their parents and exhibited the kind of love for Jesus that impacted them so when they attended church we could spend more time going deeper rather than the superficial overviews." —Urban Virginia

"There would be more activities for males. They have junior high and senior high girls' night out, but nothing for boys. My older son attends things at his friends' church, i.e. basketball games, because there isn't that opportunity at our church. There would be more low-cost events—many of the ones they offer are pricey." —Suburban Nebraska

"Educate and energize parents about their faith." —Suburban Maryland

"Participation by parents—I feel like a babysitter so the parents can go elsewhere." —Urban Ohio

"Better communication to leaders and better communication to the parents." —Suburban Missouri

Part 5—Other Volunteers

"More training available for the volunteers and having more youth involvement in church activities." —Rural Illinois

"Better notification of responsibilities prior to events." —Suburban Indiana

"I would more actively be on the recruitment trail continuously for more volunteers, not just when a perceived need arises. Also, I would use more activities that typically are more 'fun' for youth to allow visitors and friends to come more to 'relaxed' settings."
—Suburban Kentucky

Part 6—"Those Above"

"I would have them sit in the church service when we have missionary speakers, and I would have them do more Christian services." —Rural Michigan

"We really don't have budget from the church so we rely on fundraisers and the generosity of the members to support them. We also have to share our room with others especially around rummage sale time." —Suburban Ohio

"That there would be Christian education funds to train youth workers to serve well and be regularly encouraged. (Training costs so much and is usually states away.)" —Suburban North Carolina

"A pastor that is more in tune with changing worldviews. At least being aware that world view affects *how* we should teach/preach would be a help. Instead, he tends to be of the opinion that postmodern thought should be stopped." —Suburban Georgia

"More pastor involvement and understanding of comprehensive youth ministry." —Suburban Colorado

"Active participation of the pastor with the kids—not every week but enough that they know who he is."—Suburban Iowa